TUBBING
How to Plan, Build, and Use Your Hot Tub

TUBBING

How to Plan, Build,

and Use Your Hot Tub

by John Silversmith

Special Photography by Matthew Barr

Drawings by Tom Adams

Crown Publishers, Inc.   New York

Inquiries should be addressed to Crown Publishers, Inc., One Park Avenue,
New York, N.Y. 10016
Printed in the United States of America
Published simultaneously in Canada by
General Publishing Company Limited

Library of Congress Cataloging in Publication Data

Silversmith, John
Tubbing: how to plan, build, and use your hot tub.

1. Baths, Hot.   I. Title.
TH4761.S54   644'.6   78-27716
ISBN 0-517-53606-4
ISBN 0-517-53607-2 pbk

Contents

Acknowledgments

My thanks to the manufacturers of hot tub and spa kits, especially Country Comfort of Concord, California, and Barrel Builders of Lodi, California, who gave freely of their time and information about their products. And a large note of gratitude to my editor, Mimi Koren, who helped put this book in its final form.

1. Hot Tubs and You

Whether you call them hot tubs or spas, whether you use them for therapeutic reasons or simply for pleasure, the soothing effects—both physical and emotional—of hot tubs are extravagantly helpful in the daily scheme of living. The immersion of the body in hot water soothes the muscles and warms the spirits; coupled with the cleansing and the social camaraderie (optional), hot tubs make good sense.

Why not simply soak in a bathtub and let it go at that? Quite simply, the bathtub is poorly designed and difficult to use, contributes little to good health, and generally is not conducive to the good vibes received from soaking and steeping in hot tubs. There is an immense difference

9

OPPOSITE: Not all tubs are round; here is a handsome rectangular tub made of wood with a practical fiberglass liner. The tub, approximately 40 inches deep, is partially sunk in a wooden deck attached to the house. Photo courtesy Country Comfort Redwood Tubs

between the hot tub and the bathtub. If you are not convinced, try a hot tub. I did and became a firm believer, mainly because the hot tub provides:

1. Constant water temperature.
2. No need to refill or fiddle with knobs.
3. More comfort than a bathtub.
4. More emotional reward, especially if the hot tub is in a natural setting, such as outdoors.

Basic Hot Tub System

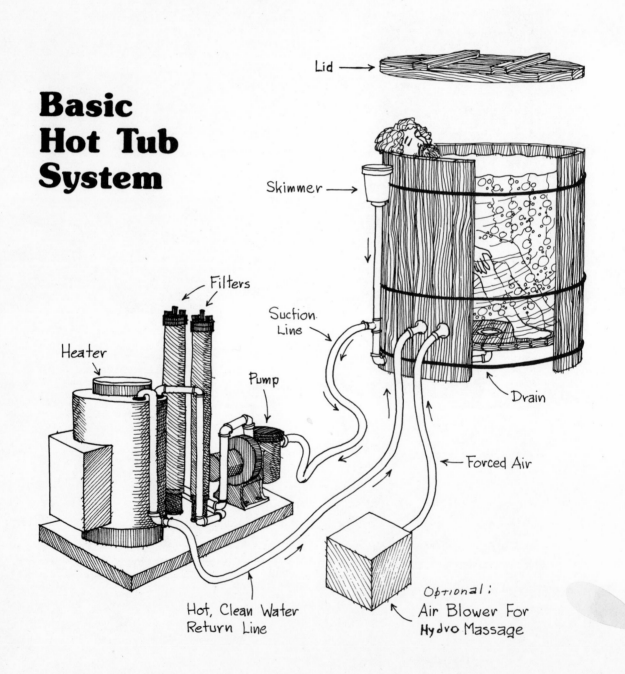

Lid

Skimmer

Filters

Heater

Pump

Suction Line

Drain

Forced Air

Hot, Clean Water Return Line

Optional: Air Blower For Hydro Massage

What Is a Hot Tub?

A hot tub is a wooden or fiberglass watertight container from 4 to 8 feet in diameter and 3 to 4 feet deep. The water in the tub is maintained at a constant temperature (usually 105 degrees F) and exudes relaxing moist steam; rather than draining off as in a traditional bathtub, it is filtered and recirculated for continuous use. No soap is used—the point is not to remove dirt (you can do that in a shower) but to soak. You can stand in a hot tub or sit on benches within the tub with your body immersed up to the neckline.

Some hot tubs are elaborate, with whirlpool jets and massaging waters, and others are simply old converted wine or rain barrels. You can build a tub yourself for minimal cost (about $400), or buy one in ready-to-assemble kit form. All hot tubs have a pump to recirculate the water and a heating device; they may have other, more sophisticated heating equipment as well.

While most hot tubs are round, some recent ones are square or rectangular. The tubs from Country Comfort of San Francisco, California, have a leakproof insulated fiberglass shell sheathed in redwood—very handsome.

A Glance at the Past

The Egyptians, Greeks, and Romans never went a day without their hot soaks in luxurious pools; to them this was a form of relaxation and therapy, where the ills of the body were banished by steaming waters. When bathing fell into disfavor in European society, all the beauty and luxury of the steaming tub was lost. Queen Isabella of Spain and various kings of England considered water on the body worse than a scourge of locusts. But in the seventeenth century, bathing made a comeback: in opulent small tubs, which unfortunately only the rich could enjoy.

In early America the bath was not considered essential to the daily scheme of things. Puritans, clean of mind, were often dirty of body. Puritan men and women kept themselves fully garbed at all times; the very idea of the bath appalled them. Perhaps the idea of sitting naked in a pool of soothing water was too sensual for them; they may have feared that it would encourage sexual promiscuity.

At the start of the nineteenth century there was a great move toward the concept of therapeutic waters. Steam baths, medicinal waters, and mud baths were all the vogue in the fashionable resorts of, for example, West Virginia. There, the Greenbrier Hotel and The Homestead became famous when doctors started to extol the virtues of a soothing warm bath. The curative waters of the grand resorts attracted a large clientele for almost three decades, but in the meantime, the bathtub became a standard fixture in homes of the rich.

The Japanese Bath

If we look at the Japanese baths called *ofuros,* in use for centuries, we can get a good idea of why hot tubs are so popular. While Americans may lunge for a martini at the end of a working day, the Japanese plunge into a hot tub. They would not consider the day complete without a good hot soak. For the Japanese, hot tubbing is therapeutic and regenerative; it provides relaxation and also (perhaps more than in America) sociability. Japanese tubbers are, from all the evidence, tough—they like their tub water at 115 degrees and sometimes more! For a Westerner, using water so hot would probably be more torture than pleasure, however.

The Japanese have for centuries believed that conversation in a cauldron of steaming water extinguishes all social barriers—when one is nude, who can tell the social distinctions? Washing is done in a separate room from the hot tub, and the bather leaves wearing very little clothing, even in winter.

Finnish Saunas

Whereas the magic of tubbing depends on hot water (wet heat), the sauna relies basically on dry heat—and has for over two thousand years. In Finland, where the sauna originated, the sauna is used as both a method of cleaning and a way to regain one's strength after a hard day's work.

In tubs you sit submerged in hot water; in saunas you sit in a wooden room luxuriating in the dry heat. The heat emanates from an assemblage of rocks and stones that have previously been heated over a wood fire. Since in the sauna the body is not actually immersed in hot water, it can withstand much higher temperatures than it can in the hot tub (190 degrees to 200 degrees F is the perfect range).

To receive the maximum benefits a sauna can afford, the Finns use it in three stages. The first stage consists solely of dry heat, which produces a profuse sweating after a short period of time. In the second stage, moist heat is produced by pouring water over the heated stones. A cold and invigorating shower is the ideal conclusion to this process. As with tubbing, a session in a sauna offers both relaxation and social conviviality.

The typical Finnish sauna is generally a single-room log building usually located away from the house; bathers undress in the home and walk nude to the sauna. Some saunas, however, function as both a steam and a wash room. The basic materials needed are fire, air, water, and stones. As in hot tub bathing, a sauna speeds circulation and raises body temperatures; the heat relieves body aches and pains and actually produces some of the benefits of exercise without requiring any movement.

Why Not the Swimming Pool?

You might think that a person could get the same effects from a dip in the pool as from a hot tub. That's only partially true. The swimming pool is essentially a vehicle for exercise, not relaxation. And it is not heated hot enough to provide soothing steam.

In addition, a swimming pool is very costly to install and requires a great deal of space and apparatus. It also needs regular maintenance, which can be expensive. Most people cannot afford to have their own swimming pool. Even if they could, the investment is often not worth the effort because of the short swimming season—three to four months at best. In contrast, the hot tub is much less expensive to install and maintain, and it can be used for five or six months, or more, in cold climates if installed with some protective screening. There are even stalwart folks who use hot tubs in midwinter—but I must admit they are rare.

Can Anyone Hot Tub?

I have seen tiny toddlers and folks in their eighties enjoying the heat of the hot tub. Almost anyone can use the tub, but the degree of heat and the length one stays in should be determined by the individual's general health. People who have had strokes or heart problems should always check with their doctor before starting any new activity. And children should never be allowed in the tub without adult supervision. Generally, however, almost anyone can submerge and enjoy the soothing benefits. (For more about how to use your tub, see Chapter 10.)

OPPOSITE: A simple wooden structure encloses this hot tub; the door at left enters directly into the house. The tub is partially sunken. Note the seating platform and pegs on walls for hanging towels. Photo by Matthew Barr

2. Types of Hot Tubs

Initially, the hot tub was made strictly of wood, and many hot tub fans still maintain that nothing is better than the beauty of, say, polished oak or redwood. I have to admit that I agree—the graining and color are stunning. But thousands of hot tub users swear by the fiber-glass tub or spa because it is easy to install, easy to clean, maintains temperature better, and prevents any possibility of leakage. Just what material you choose for your hot tub is a matter of personal taste.

In the early days, all hot tubs were free-standing units; that is, you climbed a ladder to get into them. Today, many tubs are sunken or built flush with a deck or terrace, creating a harmonious picture. And where once hot tubs were strictly for outdoors, today they are indoors as well.

OPPOSITE: Sunk about 1 foot below the deck, a conventional round tub is partially surrounded by a 2-foot platform for sitting and holding towels and potted plants. Photo by Matthew Barr

This free-standing tub in its own wooden enclosure is another variation of the round-tub design. A ladder provides easy access to the tub, which is partially surrounded by a wooden platform. Photo by Matthew Barr

Wood

It is tough to beat the beauty of teak, oak, redwood, or cedar in a hot tub. Each wood has beautiful grain, and of course wood is a natural material, which makes it appropriate for the natural act of bathing. However, wood needs maintenance, even in ideal situations. Even redwood, which lasts for some time without protection, eventually does need help to withstand the weather.

Tubs built of wood are limited to two basic shapes: round and rectangular. Their sizes may vary, from standard size to low profile. The low profile round tub is only 2½ feet high and comes in diameters of 5,

6, 7, or 8 feet. In this tub the bathers sit directly on the floor, with their feet extended, as in a bathtub. This style provides bathers with direct, close range hydromassage. It is unobtrusive and can provide the look of a sunken tub where sinking a tall tub is financially or structurally prohibitive.

The standard round hot tub, which is 4 feet high, comes in 4-, 5-, 6-, 7-, or 8-foot diameters. It has a bench around the perimeter for seating and is deep enough for bathers to stand in if they want to. It can hold more people than the low profile tub. Here is a rundown of sizes and weights for round tubs from the California Hot Tub Company:

Dimensions of Round Wood Tubs

Diameter (feet)	Height (feet)	Water Capacity (gallons)	Approx. Weight (pounds) Tub and Water		People Capacity
			Empty	Max.Cap.*	
4	4	305	2,100	2,700	2–3
5	2½	275	2,280	3,030	4–5
5	4	475	3,270	4,470	6–8
6	2½	400	3,320	4,520	6–8
6	4	700	5,810	7,460	8–10
7	2½	585	4,855	6,355	8–10
7	4	960	7,970	9,770	10–12
8	2½	705	5,850	7,650	10–12
8	4	1,230	10,210	12,310	12–14

* Estimated at 150 lbs./person

Square wood tubs, also quite beautiful, cost somewhat more than round ones. They are available from Country Comfort of Concord, California. This specific tub has some unique features: a leakproof foam-filled fiberglass outer tub that invisibly envelopes the handcrafted redwood inner tub. The durable reinforced outer layer lets you partially or fully recess the tub without fear of rot, and the outer reinforcement makes aboveground installation easy—eliminating the need for backfill or an air space underneath.

Free-standing Tubs

Free-standing vertical wooden tubs may not be as attractive as sunken ones or those encased in wooden decks. However, the free-standing tub is less expensive and easier to install, and there are ways to design the surroundings so that the tub blends in rather than looking like an afterthought. A balanced, harmonious design can be created by enclosing the area around the tub with similar vertical elements. Wing walls—simple wooden fences that match the height of the tub—are a good idea for both appearance and privacy (if modesty is one of your concerns). Trellises are a charming decorative addition.

If you are putting the tub on level ground or on a concrete patio, no further construction is needed; simply install joists and be sure there is air space between the floorboards of the tub and the ground or patio floor.

To cover the somewhat bare look of the free-standing tub, consider using container plants—even a single large specimen tree in a decorative pot can add dimension to the setting and eliminate a sterile look. In Chapter 7 we discuss various types of greenery for tub locations.

Sunken Tubs

The handsome sunken wooden tub can either extend about 20 inches above the platform or rest flush with it, with a 2-inch lip. As with a swimming pool, this enables you to step into the water rather than climbing into it. Very handsome arrangements are possible with sunken tubs, as you can see in the pictures and drawings.

Sunken-tub construction is rather time-consuming and obviously more costly than setting an upright round hot tub on joists. But if you can

OPPOSITE: A deck was built adjacent to a house to accommodate a fiberglass tub that is set flush with the wooden structure. Photo courtesy Avalon Spas

A brick patio provides a lovely setting for an octagonal fiberglass tub equipped with hydrojets—note the foaming water. Photo © Riviera Spas. Used with permission

afford it, I would certainly suggest a sunken tub for your property. (Many new homes are being built with sunken hot tubs in deck or garden settings.) The sunken or flush installation of a tub on a deck or platform creates a smooth, unified design, particularly if the deck surrounding the tub is connected to the house. The tub sunk in a deck also offers greater comfort, since the deck provides easy access from the house to the bathing spot.

Fiberglass

Fiberglass tubs (sometimes called spas) come in many shapes and sizes to match any design or opening. They are generally made of rigid polyurethane, although other types of plastic can be used. They are easy to clean, do not leak, and since they are of one piece, can be installed like a bathtub. Depending on the manufacturer, fiberglass tubs come equipped with hydrojets. Whirlpools or Jacuzzi-type machines are also

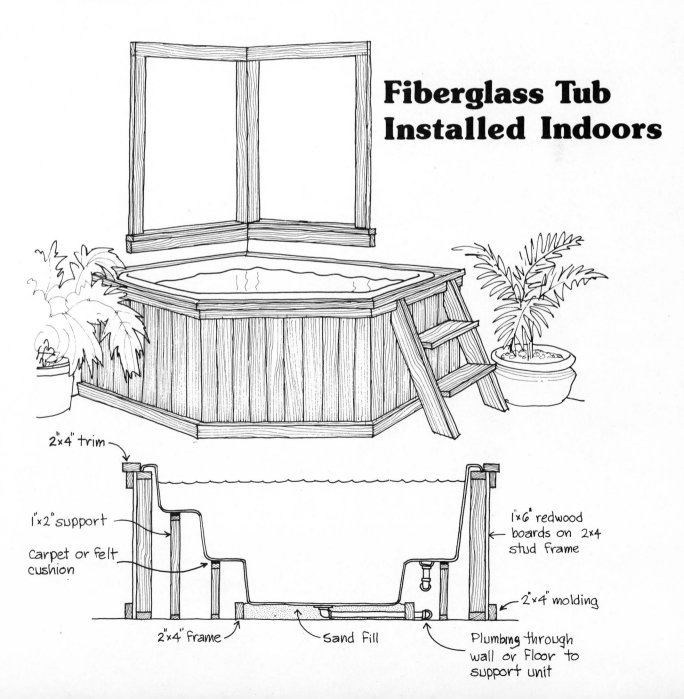

Fiberglass Tub Installed Indoors

2"x4" trim

1"x2" support

Carpet or felt cushion

1"x6" redwood boards on 2x4 stud frame

2"x4" molding

2"x4" frame

Sand Fill

Plumbing through wall or floor to support unit

used with some tubs. There is such a variety of water-circulating devices that it is impossible to list them all or discuss the advantages or disadvantages of each system. You will have to shop around and decide for yourself which jet system best suits your purposes.

As mentioned, the type of fiberglass used depends upon the manufacturer. Here are some specifications for the Avalon Spa: It is

Fiberglass Tub Installed Outdoors

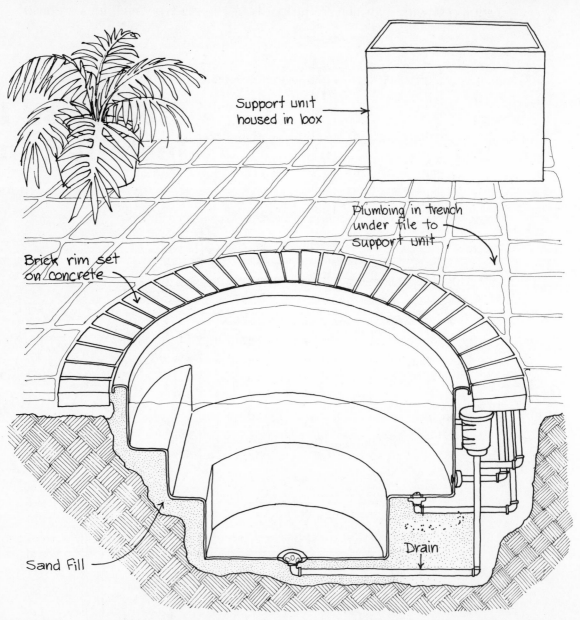

Support unit housed in box

Plumbing in trench under tile to support unit

Brick rim set on concrete

Sand Fill

Drain

made of deluxe urethane foam, with a triple-wall construction for maximum strength and insulation with minimum weight. It has a nonskid finish on the horizontal surface and the highest gel coat finish on the walls to provide a glossy smooth and durable surface. The spa can be installed aboveground or flush with it, indoors or out. Several models are currently available.

Permits and Codes

When the first hot tubs were installed by the courageous few, not much thought was given to safety requirements; the tubs were considered simply another pleasure package. But as they began to proliferate like mushrooms and as manufacturers sprang up like weeds, cities took notice. As usual, they were in a quandary over what to do about these wooden water giants. Were they swimming pools? No. So swimming pool rules could not apply. Were they bathtubs? No. So indoor plumbing codes could not apply. What were they? And, more importantly, what was to be done to be sure they were built properly and without hazard?

Regardless of how idiotic the bureaucracy surrounding building codes may seem, certain safety rules for hot tubs must be observed. Building codes for hot tubs have recently gone into effect in most areas, and permits are now necessary before you can build. Of course, that is going to cost you some money. But don't fight city hall. Let them make their inspections; let them make their suggestions because in the long run you will benefit, despite the extra cost.

With building codes in effect, at least you will have someone to consult regarding the safety of hot tub installations. It is crucial that wiring and plumbing be installed properly to protect bathers from accidents. The same is true of fence regulations, like those in force for swimming pools in California. Don't argue. Listen and ask. And since you will be paying for it, ask and be confident that when your tub is installed it is installed properly and within building codes.

3. Building Your Own Hot Tub

Why make your own hot tub when you can buy one? Because it will be cheaper, and, as with all handmade items, it will look more distinctive. It is not a job for everyone. It takes some know-how and time (a few friends help, too)—but it is definitely worth the effort. In this chapter we tell you how to build a hot tub, either starting from scratch or using the materials of an old water tower or barrel. Read the instructions through and be sure that you understand them thoroughly before you begin to work.

The reward for making your own hot tub is not only being able to say, "I made it myself," but also being able to work with wood—a heady experience. When worked properly in the hands of even the

OPPOSITE: A simple round wooden tub, set on a deck, is enhanced by finely crafted wooden steps and platform. Photo by Matthew Barr

amateur carpenter, redwood, teak, oak, and cedar can be lovely woods with beautiful graining.

Your tub need not be the conventional 8-foot diameter type but may be smaller or larger. It does not have to be of redwood. You can use plywood, for example, for an inexpensive and adequate tub for the family; or if you are really ambitious you can build a concrete tub.

Just what you decide to make depends upon your uses for the tub: will it be used frequently or just occasionally? how many people will be in it at the same time—two, four, more?

No matter what kind of distinctive tub you build, remember that it will need filters and heaters. (See chapter 5.) It is extremely important to install these correctly. For this job you might want to hire a plumber, who can probably accomplish the job in an hour or two.

As with any tub installation, be sure to check local building codes before you start.

If building your own tub seems beyond your ability or patience, then buy a prefab or kit tub. (See chapter 4.) If you don't want to assemble the kit yourself, you can usually have the manufacturer or dealer suggest a carpenter, who can do it for you (for a fee).

Preparing the Site

No matter whether you find an old tub, make one yourself, or build one from a kit, you will have to prepare the site for it. This may sound formidable, but it is not. It amounts simply to clearing the land and making a level area for your tub. (You can, of course, have someone do this for you, but that will increase your costs.) The key word here is *level* —without it, you may find the hot tub installation more of a chore than a charm.

The two conventional ways of supporting a wood tub are (1) on a slab footing or (2) on piers; either of these may be used to hold the 3 x 6-

inch joists on which the floorboards of the tub will rest. To level the site for a slab, begin by digging it out; that takes more muscle than brains. Once that is accomplished (try to get a friend to help) tamp it down. Use a carpenter's tool called a level to check out the ground. If the area is not level, rake, shovel, or walk on it until it is.

Laying the Foundation

The supports for the tub are similar to the foundation wall of a house and must be strong because the hot tub will hold from 300 to 1,200 gallons of water. The floorboards of the tub rest on joists laid on piers or a concrete slab. You will need the following materials: shovel; 3 x 6's; carpenter's level; concrete mixer (if preparing concrete yourself); chicken wire; scrap lumber—1 x 6-inch boards and 2 x 4-inch sticks; precast piers; hammer; nails; three joists, 3 x 6 inches or 4 x 4 inches each.

To lay a concrete slab foundation, make a form from scrap 1 x 6-inch boards to hold the concrete slab—at least 4 inches deep. (See drawing.) Nail the boards at the corners and secure them in place at the sides with battens (small 2 x 4-inch sticks) stuck in the ground and nailed to the boards. Inside the form place a layer of chicken wire; this helps to hold the concrete in place and keeps it from cracking. The next step is to pour the concrete; you will need a 4-inch-deep bed approximately 18 inches wider and larger than the size of the longest joist.

If you are handy, you can make the concrete yourself in a rented gasoline-powered mixer. If you would rather save the time, order the concrete and have it poured. Once the concrete is set (in about 48 hours), the wooden forms are discarded. Now lay the joists parallel and centered. They must be cut to fit inside the diameter of the tub and support its floor.

Preparing the Site

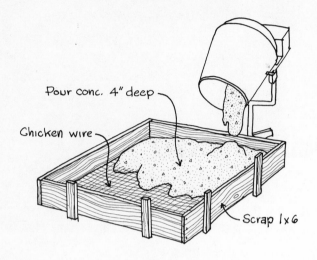

Pour conc. 4" deep

Chicken wire

Scrap 1x6

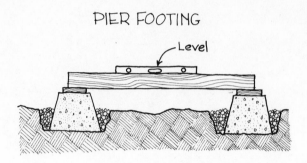

PIER FOOTING

Level

Excavate for Sloping Site

SLAB FOOTING

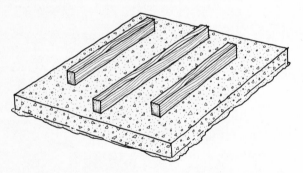

Place 3x6s on slab so air circulates under tub.

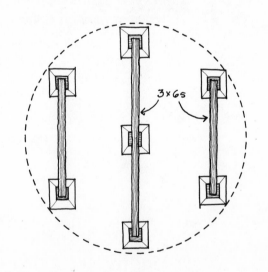

3x6s

Footing for Round Tub

If you dislike digging and don't want to tackle the concrete slab installation, or if your property is hilly, use pier footings. These are available ready-made at suppliers. Mark holes and spacing for piers; they must be placed to fit inside the diameter of the tub. Space on 2-foot centers as shown in the drawing. Dig holes for the piers; level the bottom of the holes. Install the piers in a generous puddle of concrete. To make sure that they are set into the holes level, place a board across the tops and set a carpenter's level on it. Once the concrete puddles have set, place three joists on top of the piers, as shown in the drawing. Again get out the level and be sure the joists are level throughout. You will need four or more piers to support the conventional round tub.

There are other ways of preparing a foundation—with a bed of coarse gravel, for example, with joists laid directly on the gravel. While this is inexpensive it is not always successful and can make drainage a problem. It's best to do it the right way with suitable foundations so that you don't find yourself floating down the garden.

Building a Wood Tub from Scratch

If you are reasonably handy with tools and like to work with wood, you may be able to build a hot tub from scratch. It is a challenging task but certainly not an impossible one. And it will save you a lot of money—as much as $200 to $500 off the cost of purchasing a kit. So let's look at the basics of building a hot tub.

Once you have laid the foundation, you are ready to buy the wood. Clear all-heart redwood is what you want; this grade of lumber does not have knots and has a straight vertical grain. Teak or cedar will do just as well but may be harder to obtain and somewhat more expensive. Basically, the hot tub is made of staves (boards) for the sides; 2 x 10-inch boards for the bottom; and joists and piers to set it on. (The sizes depend on the size of the tub you are building.) You will also need lugs, nuts, and hoops (usually ⅜-inch iron rods threaded on both sides); some mastic or roofing compound (to be used sparingly); ⅜-inch dowels (18 inches' worth for each floorboard); some nails; and some scrap wood strips.

Read the instructions through carefully and consult the drawings before you begin.

Do the floor of the tub first—this is easy and gets you off to a good start. Use 2 x 10-inch boards; do the dowel work first. Mark holes for drilling; be sure marks are lined up perfectly to match the adjoining boards. Drill three holes on each side of each piece, but on one side only of two end pieces spaced equidistant from each other; drill straight and true with a ⅜-inch drill (a power drill is fastest). Then cut out 3-inch lengths of ⅜-inch dowels, which will serve as pegs. Fit them into the holes; they must fit securely.

It is a good idea to spread some mastic or sealer on the edges of the boards before you dowel them together, but only a little mastic—keep it off the top of the boards so it does not ooze out and create an oil slick when water is in the tub. Fit the doweled boards together and then tack them down with two 1 x 3-inch wood strips laid flat—use ¾-inch nails so you won't pierce the boards. When the mastic is dry (an hour or so) and boards tacked in place, turn over the floorboards and scribe a circle—the size depends on what size tub you want. Then cut the circle carefully with a hand coping saw or a jigsaw (much faster). Sand the edges of the boards until they are smooth, tapering the circumference.

Next, cut the staves (sides) of the tub to length, 4 feet or whatever height you have chosen. Here comes the hard part: You must bevel the edges of the boards at an angle of about 6½ degrees. Do this with a radial arm saw, beveling both edges so that they will form a V on the outside of the tub when they are placed side by side. Then cut out a ¾-inch groove about 4 inches from the bottom of the boards. This will hold the 2 x 10 floorboards on the inside face. The groove should be slightly narrower than their width. (See drawing.)

When you have finished cutting all the staves, it is time for the moment of truth—putting them together. The foundation joists should already be in place. (See preceding section on laying the foundation.) Set the floorboards at right angles to the joists, but do not nail them down. Put a very thin coating of mastic on the outer edge of the floorboards, but keep the inner third of the board clean. Apply a thin coat of mastic also to the edge of the first prepared stave, and set the stave to span a joint between two floorboards. Tap it in place, using a sledgehammer against a wood block so as not to mar the staves. Proceed likewise with the remaining staves, tapping each halfway in place and fitting them tightly to each other. You will have to cut the last stave to fit the width.

To bind the tub you will need the hoops; put the lowest hoop about 4 inches from the bottom. Bend the rod around the tub, slip the threaded ends through a lug, and loosely screw on the nuts and washers—do not tighten. Do the same with the other two hoops. When the hoops are all placed, tighten each lug, starting at the bottom. Now pound the staves firmly against the floorboards.

Treating the Finished Tub

Unless you are installing a commercial kit hot tub that already has been treated with preservatives, you will have to treat the wood to protect it from weathering. The best thing to use is linseed oil, applied in a single coat on the outside of your tub once a year. This preserves the wood and keeps the steel hoops free from rust.

A tub made of new redwood may release tannin into the water, which gives the water a rusty look. If you drain the tub and add several

Round Tub Construction

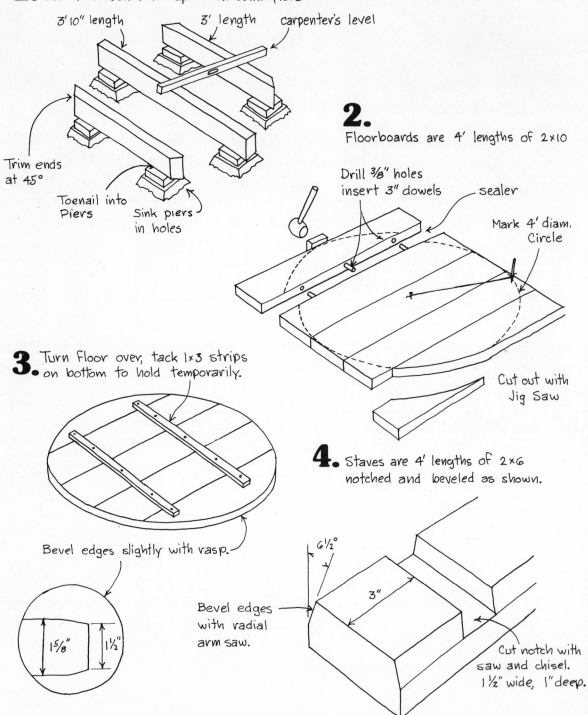

1. Set 4 × 6 Joists 16" apart on conc. piers

3' 10" length

3' length

carpenter's level

Trim ends at 45°

Toenail into Piers

Sink piers in holes

2.

Floorboards are 4' lengths of 2×10

Drill 3/8" holes insert 3" dowels

sealer

Mark 4' diam. Circle

Cut out with Jig Saw

3. Turn Floor over, tack 1×3 strips on bottom to hold temporarily.

Bevel edges slightly with rasp.

1 5/8"   1 1/2"

4. Staves are 4' lengths of 2×6 notched and beveled as shown.

6 1/2°

3"

Bevel edges with radial arm saw.

Cut notch with saw and chisel. 1 1/2" wide, 1" deep.

5.

Pound staves onto
floorboards at notch.
This should be a very
tight fit.

← Temporary 1"x2"

6.

Put roofing compound
in joints for sealing but
leave inside surfaces
clean so as not to
pollute water.

Use wire to
hold temporarily

Use rasp to
cut groove for hoops.

7.

Lugs

Hoops are 14' lengths of ⅜" diam.
iron rod. Use small nails to hold
temporarily in place.

8. Before tightening hoops with foundry
lugs, check alignment and fit of pieces.

Sand all edges
drill necessary holes
for plumbing.

6"

23"

16"

3"

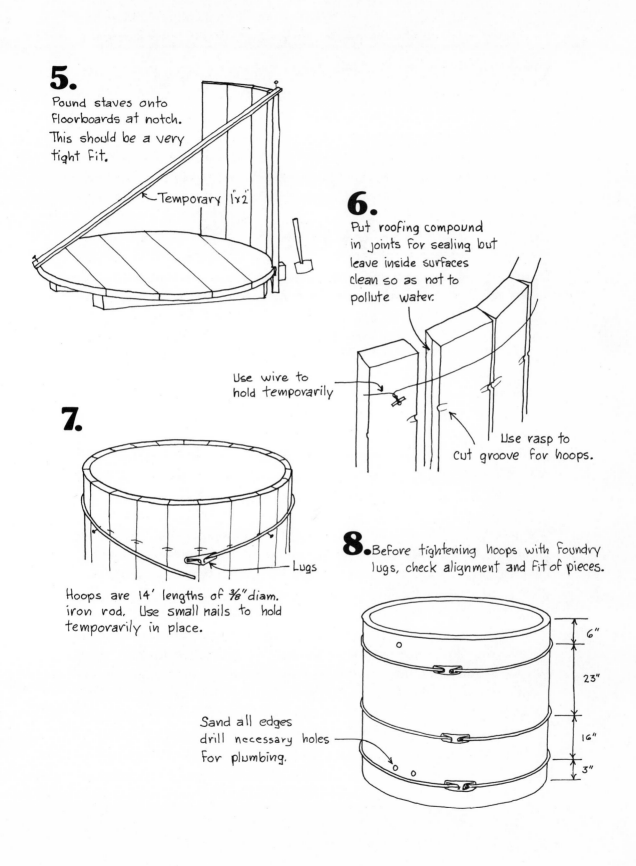

changes of fresh water, the tannin will eventually disappear. Or you could use prebleached wood rather than redwood to completely avoid this problem.

Salvaged Water Tanks and Wine Barrels

A big old water tank that someone has abandoned could become your hot tub. Unfortunately, old water tanks are not easy to find. Drive through the country and make inquiries, or call some friends who might have seen one. Watch classified ads in local newspapers, too. Once you locate such a tank, contact the owner of the property and ask if it is possible to salvage the tub. The chances are slim, but if you do find one—then what?

Assemble as many friends as you can and dismantle the tank. This will take time and ingenuity. I do not recommend moving the tank in one piece, for chances are you do not have access to a truck large enough to carry it. It is better to dismantle the tank and put it together later. You will need a red crayon, a heavy crescent wrench, a plumber's pliers, and a product called Liquid Wrench. Before you disassemble the tank, take the crayon and number all staves (vertical pieces) in sequence. Old water tanks (and wine barrels, too) have staves with bevels. The staves are not identical, so it is imperative to mark each stave in sequence; otherwise you will have a difficult time reassembling them. Also mark the floor planking (these boards also vary) and the barrel hoops. Douse the nuts and bolts that hold the hoops with Liquid Wrench, wait twenty minutes, and then use the wrench or pliers to remove the hoops. Put all the pieces in a truck and get to your house before the person you bought the tank from decides he wants to build his own hot tub.

To assemble the tub, lay out a foundation for it as previously described and then set down and reassemble floorboard, staves, and hoops. Use the preceding instructions for building a tub from scratch as a guideline.

You can still find old wine barrels, especially in wine-making country; they make fine hot tubs. They come in many sizes, some so huge it is not feasible to use them, but most are of moderate size, just right for four people. Again, the best procedure is to dismantle the barrel and reassemble it once you have it on home grounds. You will have to bleach out the wood to eliminate wine residue and acids and odor. To do this, stir one cup of chlorine into the water and allow it to sit for 48 hours.

Soaking in a good hot tub—as in this rectangular one of finely crafted redwood—can be an exhilarating experience. The wide ledge is ideal for holding refreshments, towels, and other accouterments. Photo courtesy Country Comfort Redwood Tubs

Simple Plywood Tub

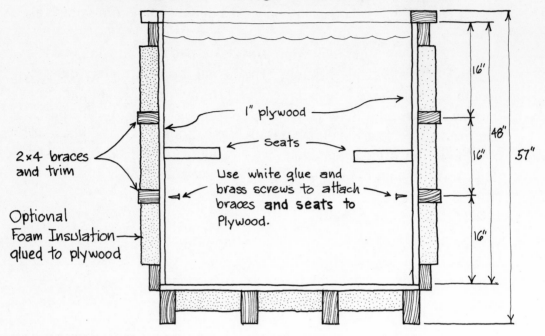

2×4 braces and trim

1" plywood

Seats

Use white glue and brass screws to attach braces **and seats** to Plywood.

Optional Foam Insulation glued to plywood

16"

16"

16"

48"

57"

SECTION VIEW

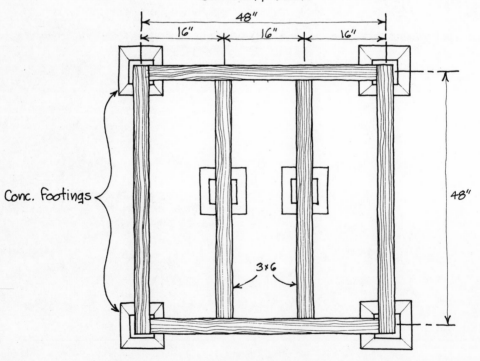

48"

16"   16"   16"

Conc. footings

3×6

48"

JOIST PLAN

Plywood Tubs

With the new wood epoxies and glues, glazing compounds, and waterproofing products available, it is now possible to build a hot tub out of plywood. This is not the conventional hot tub—round and made of redwood—but it can be made easily by anyone with a basic knowledge of carpentry. The installation is not difficult; you can do it in a weekend with a little help from friends—especially if you tell them they can use it, too. (See drawings for construction details.)

This tub is made of 1-inch marine plywood, set on piers; it can be used on the patio or in the garden. Landscaped with suitable greenery, it can be a handsome addition to the property. The plywood tub is basically a box glued at the corners and braced with 2 x 4's secured at corners with L brackets. The joists, 3 x 6-inch boards, are supported by six precast concrete piers available at lumberyards. The piers have wooden inserts and the joists are toenailed to the piers.

You will need the following materials:

5 pieces	4 x 4-foot plywood, 1 inch thick (marine grade)
1	2 x 10-inch redwood bench
6	3 x 6-inch redwood joists, cut to size
12	2 x 4-inch approximately 4 feet long, miter cut
4	1 x 3-inch x 48-inch mouldings
4	Concrete piers
12	L Brackets

Brass screws
White glue
Sealant

For the cover of the tub you will need:

1	4 x 4-foot plywood (marine grade), 1 inch thick
4	2 x 4-inch boards
1	4 x 4-foot foam insulation, 1 inch thick

Simple Plywood Tub

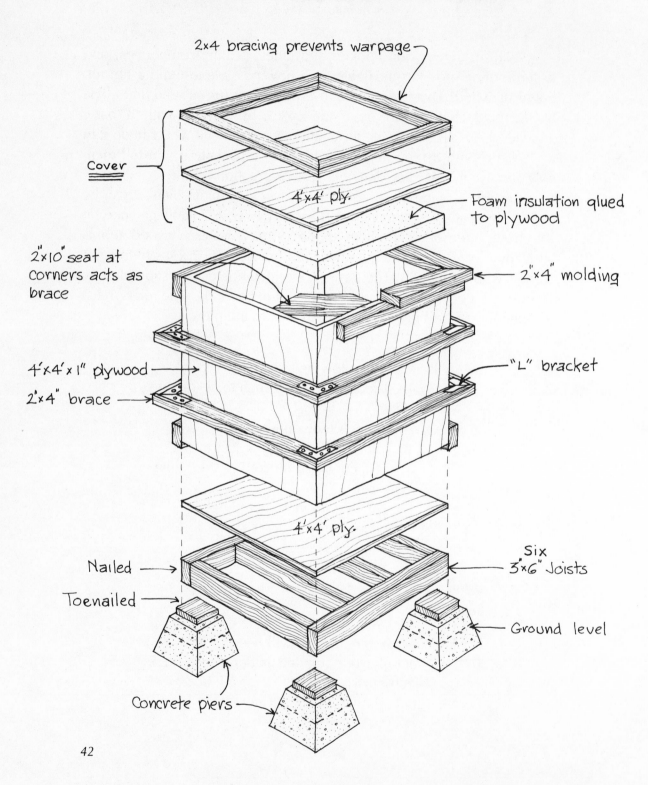

2x4 bracing prevents warpage

Cover

4'x4' ply.

Foam insulation glued to plywood

2"x10" seat at corners acts as brace

2"x4" molding

4'x4'x1" plywood

2"x4" brace

"L" bracket

4'x4' ply.

Nailed

Six 3"x6" Joists

Toenailed

Ground level

Concrete piers

First, prepare the site and lay the foundation with piers, as described earlier in the chapter. Set piers in place with the top 4 inches exposed. Nail the joists together and toenail them to piers as shown in the drawing. Now epoxy all sides of the plywood boards (consult package for drying time); secure the outer 2 x 4-inch braces to the plywood with white glue and brass screws. Screw L brackets in place on the 2 x 4s, and nail in place 2 x 10s for the seat. Add a 3-inch moulding at the top rim for detailing.

To make the lid, use a sheet of plywood and 2 x 4 moulding. Glue a sheet of foam insulating rubber (⅛"–½" thick) to the plywood to help keep heat in the tub when it is not in use. (See detail of cover in drawing.) You can also use foam insulation around the tub if you like; glue in place.

To further seal all corners, glaze bottom and sides with a suitable glazing compound available at hardware stores; then apply waterproof fiberglass resin; brush on evenly and allow to dry. Follow directions on packages of glazing compounds and fiberglass resin. (There are many trade names, and directions differ slightly.)

Fill the tub with water as you would for any hot tub.

A Tub for Two

Here is a simple tub for one—or two, if they are compatible people—and easy as pie to make. Make a box from 2 x 10s. Dowel and peg the corners. Then set the tub on bricks placed at each corner. Glaze the inside with resin to waterproof it, and fill the tub with water. Use hot water piped in with suitable connections to the tub. If your tub is outdoors, you can install a regular sink drain to empty it if necessary. This is certainly not the most sophisticated piece of equipment known, but it will serve its purpose.

The cost of this minitub is minimal—about $60 for lumber—and the tub can be made in a weekend. However, don't expect it to last forever; let's say it is a suitable answer until you can afford a conventional hot tub with more room and sturdier construction.

Concrete Tubs

You can buy a preformed concrete fountain-type pool to install for use as a hot tub, but it costs dearly. With a little perseverance and knowledge you can make your own in a few weekends. It should be deep enough so that when you sit in it the water will cover your shoulders. Consult the drawing for details.

You will need the following materials (the amount depends on the size of the tub you are building): string, reinforcing rods, 1-inch wire mesh, gravel, cement, sand, a concrete mixer, and a large piece of burlap.

To begin, mark out the desired shape of the pool on the ground, using some string or a pointed tool.

Excavate to about 4 feet, rake it smooth, and level the site, using a carpenter's level. The base must be absolutely firm and true to prevent the soil from sinking and causing cracks in the pool. Install drain and outlet for plumbing (you might want a professional to do this). Now cover the bottom of the site with a layer of reinforcing rods and wire mesh, available at suppliers, and anchor them into the soil. Also form the wire mesh to the sides of the site. The idea is to create binding surfaces for the concrete, so the rods and mesh can be set in almost any position.

In a rented mixer, mix 1 part cement, 2 parts sand, and 5 parts broken rubble or stone with enough water to make a fairly thick mixture. (You will need approximately 3 yards of dry cement for a pool 5 feet in diameter.) Work a 3-inch layer of this concrete into the excavation over the reinforcing material. Allow to dry somewhat (about 48 hours) and then add another 3-inch bed of concrete (using a somewhat thinner mixture). Let the concrete set a few days and then sprinkle it lightly with water.

For the sides of the pool use a thicker concrete of 1 part cement to 3 parts sand, without any aggregate. Use stones as a backfill to strengthen the face of the excavation and to provide a textured surface so that cement will adhere. Apply two layers of cement to line the sides. Make the first layer 3 inches thick and apply over the wire and allow to dry somewhat (until it is tacky). Then apply a second layer of concrete over the reinforcing wire and cover it thoroughly. Trowel it smooth.

Freeform Concrete Tub

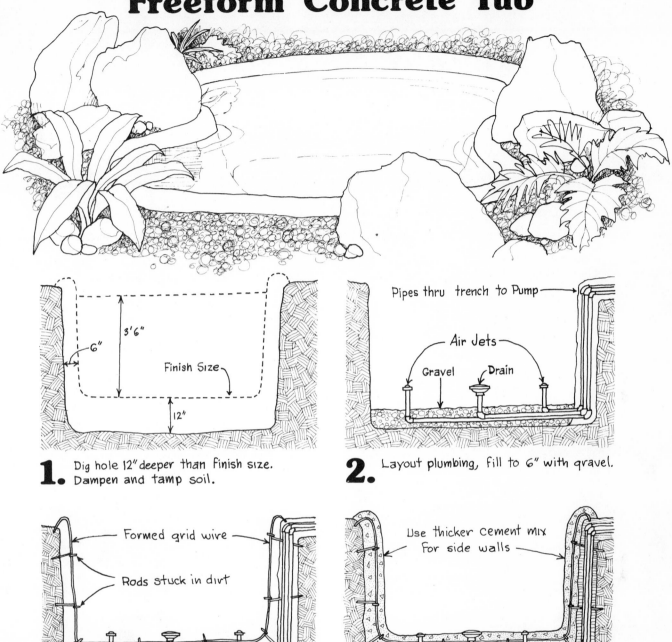

1. Dig hole 12" deeper than finish size. Dampen and tamp soil.

3'6"

6"

Finish Size

12"

2. Layout plumbing, fill to 6" with gravel.

Pipes thru trench to Pump

Air Jets

Gravel *Drain*

3. Use 2" grid wire for reinforcement. Set 3" from surface on rods.

Formed grid wire

Rods stuck in dirt

4. Pour and tamp concrete, smooth around fittings, allow to cure **48 hours**, then seal.

Use thicker cement mix for side walls

Concrete must set slowly to avoid cracks and leaks. Cover the pool with burlap, and keep the material moist for about ten days. This is necessary in order to cure the concrete and thus prevent lime—harmful to humans—from polluting the water once the pool is filled.

4. Tubs from Kits

U ntil recently, if you wanted a hot tub you had to make one from an old barrel or build one from scratch. That's not so any longer, and what a change there's been. Today there are at least 24 hot tub manufacturers throughout the United States that supply kits with all parts for a hot tub. You can put the kit together yourself or hire a carpenter to do it for you. Many times the kit manufacturers provide workers to assemble the tub at an extra charge. Kit manufacturers also furnish plumbing accessories such as heaters and pumps. You can do your own plumbing and hook-ups (not easy) or have a plumber or the kit manufacturer help you. Kit manufacturers usually furnish complete instructions and other pertinent details, which you can write for (see later in this chapter).

OPPOSITE: A clever arrangement was created for a partially sunken wooden tub built from a kit. The area is enclosed with glass and is further protected by a handsome trellis. The hand-laid tiles along the outer rim of the tub add a note of color. Assorted plants complete the scene. Photo by Matthew Barr

Some of the biggest bathtub manufacturers now have hot tub designs on their boards, and many swimming pool companies are handling them. Though more expensive than a homemade tub, hot tub kits make gorgeous tubs and are well worth the price. They come in all sorts of shapes: square, round, rectangular, octagonal, and so on, in cedar or redwood. Some have shiny preservatives; others have a beautiful natural finish.

The kit offers the advantage of convenience. It provides all the pieces knocked down (KD), ready for you to put together, not an especially difficult job. (Usually you must prepare your own foundation, as described in chapter 3.) The price of a prefab hot tub ranges from $1,000 up, depending upon the accessories and equipment. There are so many manufacturers, designs, and materials that no one manufacturer can be recommended here.

Choosing the Tub

It is best to visit suppliers in person, so that you can examine the types of wood and shapes and make an intelligent selection. If you cannot do so, send for their catalogs. Generally you can tell from pictures what is available and what will suit your needs. For example, if you have a large family or many friends, a large tub is the logical answer. If the hot tub is for you only, then a smaller tub will do.

Pay attention to personal recommendations. This is the best way to gauge the worth of a product. If you see an installation you like and the owner says it works well, take down the manufacturer's name. If you have a friend who has a prefab tub, take a trial soak.

Select a heater to meet the needs of your climate (see chapter 5 for more information), and remember to include in your figuring the cost of pumps, filters, and other amenities. Always know where your hot tub will be placed before you buy—an outdoor location might call for a different style of tub than an indoor spot. Also consider how much space you have available. If you have only 8 feet on your deck, do not purchase a 10-foot diameter tub. It is better in this case to have a smaller tub and be able to use some of the deck space. Finally, be sure the manufacturer has clear and complete instructions for all aspects of assembling the hot tub (most do).

To find prefab hot tub suppliers, consult the yellow pages of your telephone directory (larger plumbing wholesalers distribute to the smaller retailers who are listed in the phone book), newspaper and magazine ads, and people that you know. Here is a selected list of manufacturers (this is in no way an endorsement; just a sampling):

CALIFORNIA

Nordic Sauna and Hot Tub
P.O. Box 1123
Belmont, CA 94002

California Hot Tubs of Carmel
Cachague Road, Box 103
Carmel Valley, CA 93924

Country Comfort
Redwood Hot Tubs
P.O. Box 398
Concord, CA 94522

Laguna Hot Tubs
772 Newton Way
Costa Mesa, CA 92627

Stefanich Wood Tank Company
285 W. Shaw, Suite 204
Fresno, CA 93704

Joe Dunn
Sonoma Hot Tubs
P.O. Box 907
Healdsburg, CA 95448

Pacific Wood Tank
Division of Sauers Forest Products
P.O. Box 188
Healdsburg, CA 95448

The California Hot Tub Co., Inc.
3551 Haven Ave.
Menlo Park, CA 94025

Redwood Hot Tubs
227 Shoreline Highway
Mill Valley, CA 94941

Macball Industries Inc.
Dept. S 28
5765 Lowell Street
Oakland, CA 94608

The Tubmakers
2500 Market Street
Oakland, CA 94067

Avalon Spas, Inc.
612 West Katella
Orange, CA 92667

Pacific Hotbath
814 San Antonio Road
Palo Alto, CA 94303

Bauer Baths
650 S. 13th St.
Richmond, CA 94804

Barrel Builders
1085 Lodi Lane
St. Helena, CA 94574

California Cooperage
P.O. Box E, Railroad Square
San Luis Obispo, CA 93406

American Tank and Mill Company
P.O. Box 3132
Shell Beach, CA 93449

Rexford Enterprises
P.O. Box 60307
Sunnyvale, CA 94088

Riviera Spa
11735 Sheldon Street
Sun Valley, CA 91352

Aquarian Hot Tub Company
120 Stadler Drive
Woodside, CA 94062

New York

Arrow Tank Company
16 Barnett Street
Buffalo, N.Y. 14215

Sundown Hot Tubs and Saunas
696 N. Ohioville Rd.
New Paltz, N.Y. 12561

California Hot Tubs
60 Third Ave.
New York, N.Y. 10003

Oregon

National Tank and Pipe Company
10037 S.E. Mather Road
P.O. Box 7
Clackamas, Oregon 97015

Assembling the Pieces

Should you put your tub together yourself? Of course. It is not difficult, so there is no need to pay someone to do it for you. The pumps and heaters can create some problems, but if you are installing a commercial hot tub a reputable manufacturer will advise you and give you proper drawings and instructions about installing the hardware. (Or hire a plumber for this part of the installation.)

Once the foundation's ready, the do-it-yourself installation of the tub should not take more than a weekend. Have the site ready; work slowly and carefully. Have suitable tools on hand, such as hammers, mallets, screwdrivers, levels. And, of course, have a little bit of patience.

A hot tub can be set on a site, recessed in a platform, set flush with a deck, and so forth—we explore constructing decks, patios, and other apparatus in chapter 7. For now, remember that the site for any tub must be absolutely level or you will curse yourself. See chapter 3 for instructions on leveling the site and preparing the foundation. Remember that the weight of the water is held by the floorboards resting on joists laid on piers or a concrete slab. The hoops around the staves contain the water. If the weight were taken just by the staves, the floorboards would twist or crack.

Once the joists are in place, lay on them the bottom boards of the tub. Start at the center and use dowels and a good water-resistant glue. Lay the bottom boards at right angles to the joists. Smear the glue on the edge of the long sides of the boards, and then use the dowels to lock the pieces together. Lightly tap the boards together, and tack two laths across them to hold them securely during assembly. Use small nails so they do not protrude through the boards, and do not nail the bottom boards to the joists.

This constitutes the floor of the tub, and you are now ready to construct the walls. Apply mastic to the perimeter of the floor. Put the first stave in place, spanning a joint between two bottom boards. Tap the stave halfway with a mallet and a clock of scrap wood to prevent marring the stave. Let the stave outward slightly, and brace it as necessary with a piece of lath.

Put the rest of the staves in place, slightly locking them into each other and letting them lean outward slightly. On new tubs you must cut the last stave to size (to width). Mark the width accurately from the inside, at the bottom. Cut the board with a table power saw. Be sure that the last stave is cut at the same level as the others were.

Before putting on the metal hoops, tap in rows of small nails about ¼ inch below where the hoops are to go, starting 6 to 9 inches from the bottom of the tub. The nails will hold the hoops in place until you secure them. Put the lowest hoop on first, with the threaded end to the left, and install the nut and take up most of the slack. The center of the lug should span the joint between two staves. Space each successive hoop above and to the right of the preceding one, with the lugs always across two staves.

Steps give access to a tub that is set flush with the deck. The louvered fence buffers the wind and affords privacy while still providing a view.
Photo courtesy Barrel Builders

When all the hoops are in place, tighten each lug tightly and securely, starting at the bottom. Remove any bracing before doing this operation. Use a block of wood and a hammer, and round out the tank and face the staves flush on the inside with each other. Give the bottom hoops a few solid hits to drive them into the wood; this also forces the staves, not the bottom boards. Keep tightening the lugs until they are really secure.

Now you are ready to install bench planks and other accouterments. Use 2 x 10 boards cut to shape, and be sure to attach all inside woodwork with dowels and glue—no nails or screws. Predrilled holes are in place for the plumbing; it is best to have a professional do the installation. Next, fill the tub. The first filling of the tub may send you into panic because it is going to leak like a sieve, but in a few hours, as the wood swells, leaks will disappear. You can prevent this moment of despair if you wet down the outdoor tub with a sprinkler for a few hours or overnight, just as you would cure concrete. If your tub is indoors, or if the leak persists, dump in a small can of fine sawdust. The sawdust filters into cracks and crannies and seals the leaks; the excess sawdust will be removed by the filter.

A wooden tub must have water in it at all times, just like a swimming pool. When it is not in use, it is a good idea to cover it with a wooden lid, for safety's sake and to keep in the heat and keep out small animals and other critters.

The Advantages of a Kit

Are there advantages in buying a hot tub kit and putting it together (or having it put together), rather than building one from scratch? Certainly: you get a choice of tubs, you get instructions on how to install it, and you can buy all equipment in one place. Usually, the kit includes heaters, filters, and other auxiliary equipment. Most suppliers you talk to will give you all the verbal help you want and will be eager to help you get it right. However, unless the specific company has a qualified installer you will still be expected to hook up plumbing and electrical work yourself.

At this writing, there is still some debate as to which union is involved. Plumbers? Electricians? Be careful and get all the facts first: If you pay for installation, does it include the plumbing and electrical hook-up? Does it include the foundation? the actual putting together of the tub? and so on. Ask questions. There may not be anyone to rip you off, but it's worth knowing in advance what you are paying for.

The disadvantage of the hot tub kit is its cost; it is more expensive than a do-it-yourself tub, but many times it is worth paying to get the materials precut, especially if you are not handy with tools or do not have the time. Then the extra money makes sense; otherwise you are better off to save the cents and do it yourself.

In essence, it simmers down to money and just how much of it you can afford for a tub. If you have it, you can get someone to do it all for you. If you don't have it, then of course don't be without a tub; make it yourself!

The setting for this partially sunken tub is ingenious—the mechanisms of the tub are hidden in the wooden structure that surrounds it, and wooden louvers provide privacy. Decorative lookout holes are cut into the bracing at the right of the tub. Photo courtesy Barrel Builders

5. Equipment and Accessories

You could fill a rain barrel with hot water or use a wooden hot tub with water heated by the sun for a few days, but it is best to use filters and heaters for your tub. Such equipment is not particularly expensive and in the long run pays for itself in increasing your enjoyment of the tub. Just how sophisticated you get about the whole thing depends upon you and your pocketbook. Let's look at the various components available for hot tubs and which ones are essential.

Filters and Pumps

The filter is an essential part of a good hot tub; it keeps the water clean. The cartridge filter is perhaps the most popular of all filters to install and maintain: you just remove the cartridge and hose or soak it clean. Another type, using diatomaceous earth or sand as a filter, depends on a backwash system and requires permanent plumbing to flush the waste into a disposal system. Regardless of the type of filter, its size must increase as the horsepower of the pump increases, to accommodate the greater flow rate. The flow rate is determined by the number of hydrojets on the system—the more jets there are, the larger the pump must be.

A conventional pump pulls water from the tub at the rate of about 50 gallons/minute. The water passes through a heat-retaining, noncorrosive suction line to a strainer that removes dirt, hair, and lint. The pump is driven by a ½-horsepower motor that runs on 115 or 230 volts. (This is large enough to operate one jet.) The bearings of the pump are sealed and require no oiling. The horsepower of the pump depends on how many jets are used; 3 jets require a 1-horsepower pump, panel, or subpanel on its own circuit, with the appropriate circuit breaker and wire. Follow local electrical codes, or contact an electrician for installation. Always protect the pump from the outdoor elements. (See later in the chapter for suggested coverings.)

Hydrojets and Bubblers

Hydromassage or hydrotherapy jets create water movement—a massagelike action that swirls water around the body. This "massage" increases circulation of the blood and provides soothing warmth. The jets have a fully adjustable directional flow. Each jet requires a certain pump capacity. As mentioned, the size of the pump increases as you add more jets. Jets are generally installed by a plumber; they are set into

A heater and filter system connected to the tub is set on gravel and a small wooden platform. While this exposed arrangement is satisfactory, it would have been much better if the system were enclosed in its own wooden structure. Photo by Matthew Barr

predrilled holes in the tub. Two jets are adequate for a 5- or 6-foot tub.

In addition to the hydromassage jets, you can install a floor bubbler system that forces air into a perforated ring at the bottom of the tub. This system creates a steaming cauldron that some people find very enjoyable. The pump operates on 115 volts, with a load of 6 amperes.

Heaters

Most heaters for hot tub water systems operate on gas and are rated by British thermal units (Btu.). A Btu. is the amount of heat necessary to raise the temperature of 1 pound of water 1 degree F at or near 39.2 degrees F. For example, a 125,000 Btu. heater will raise a 5 x 4 tub at 60 degrees to 110 degrees in 2¼ hours; a 225,000 Btu. heater will heat up cold water in a 5 x 4 tub to 100 degrees in about 1 hour. Some heaters can be set on combustible surfaces, but others must be placed on noncombustible surfaces.

Electric heating (expensive) for hot tubs must be wired properly on its own 220-volt, 60-ampere breaker. Be certain your electrical panel can accept an additional load like this. Use this type of heating only if you can afford it; it will also serve as a supplemental source of heat along with a solar heating system.

There are many kinds of solar heaters, from single or double glazed copper or aluminum absorber panels to the plastic collector panels. These heaters catch the heat of the sun and keep the water warm. However, remember that the process works only when the sun is shining, so that an auxiliary heater is usually necessary. The subject of solar heating is so big that we cover it separately in Chapter 6.

The size of the heater determines how fast the water heats up. An 85,000 Btu. heater is usually adequate for most round tubs up to 7 feet in diameter. When controlled by a timer—the recommended method— the heater automatically replaces the small amount of heat lost over a

24-hour period; without a timer you can turn it on yourself as necessary. Whenever possible, protect the heater from the elements, especially in cold climates.

Equipment Specifications

Number of hydrotherapy jets	Size requirements Pump/filter
1 jet	½ h.p./50 gpm
2 jets	¾ h.p./50 gpm
3 jets	1 h.p./50 gpm
4 or 5 jets	1½ h.p./70 gpm

Pump/filter

H.P.	Jets	115 v.	230 v.
½	1	15	15
¾	2	20	15
1	3	25	15
1½	4	30	20
2	6	35	25

HEATERS: 85,000 Btu. is most recommended for temperate climates. Larger heaters are necessary in cold climates.

Manufacturer	Btu.	Fuel	Indoors/Outdoors
A.O. Smith	54,608	Electric	In
A.O. Smith	85,000	LP/NAT	Out
A.O. Smith	160,000	LP/NAT	In/Out
A.O. Smith	250,000	LP/NAT	In/Out
Teledyne/Laers	125,000	LP/NAT	In/Out
Teledyne/Laers	175,000	LP/NAT	In/Out

FLOOR BUBBLERS: A ½ h.p. Anzen Air Blower forces 90 C.F.M. of air into a perforated tube mounted under seats on the floor of the tub. 110 v. only, 6 amps.

TIMERS: Weather-tight timers cycle the pump on a preset basis to filter and heat your tub. Available in 115 v. or 230 v. Includes manual override switch for hydrotherapy jet operation.

Specifications are courtesy of Barrel Builders, St. Helena, CA.

Housing the Mechanisms

When equipment is being installed outdoors, a 3 x 5-foot concrete pad or its equivalent is needed for the heater, filter, and pump. If the equipment is to be indoors, leave an 18-inch clearance around the sides of the heater to keep it away from any combustible materials. A minimum of 3 feet overhead clearance is needed for all gas heaters. Indoor gas heaters all require exhaust flues.

The equipment for a hot tub can be easily hidden in suitable wood housings, as it is in swimming pools. You can build the housing yourself (see drawing); it requires little expertise once the initial electrical installations are made.

You can rig up your own heaters and filters or buy them locally from dealers, but your best bet is to purchase them from tub suppliers because they handle an array of accessories for tubs. If you buy a heater and filter first, then a bubbler later, and so on, the cost is not exorbitant. And the dealer will help you with installation if you want to tackle the job, or install it for you, or arrange to have someone else install it for you. All this depends upon your needs and budget.

Support Unit Box

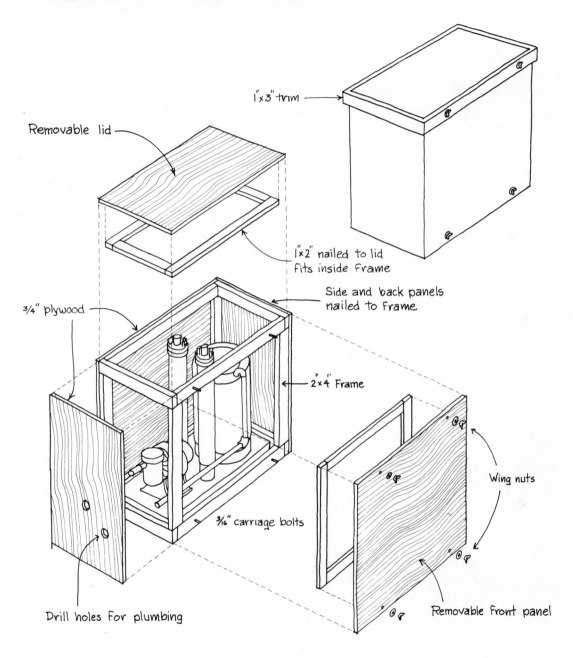

1" x 3" trim

Removable lid

1" x 2" nailed to lid
fits inside frame

Side and back panels
nailed to frame

3/4" plywood

2" x 4" Frame

Wing nuts

3/16" carriage bolts

Drill holes for plumbing

Removable front panel

63

Tops

Fit boards together, cut out circle 56" in dia.

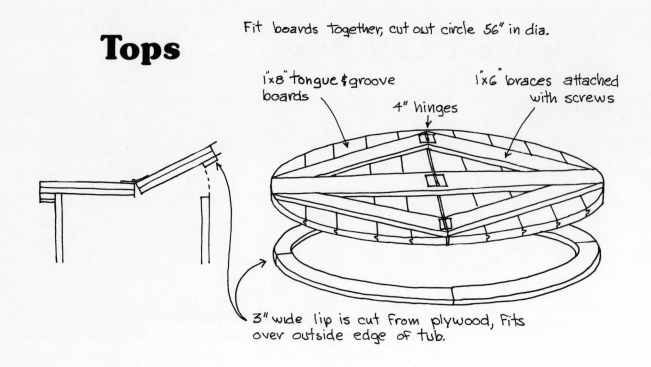

1"x8" tongue & groove boards

1"x6" braces attached with screws

4" hinges

3" wide lip is cut from plywood, fits over outside edge of tub.

Seat

Cut 2"x10" to fit inside dia. of tub.

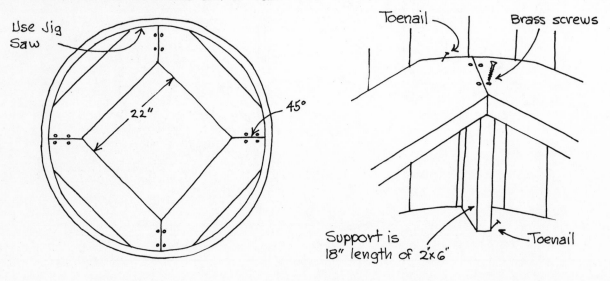

Use Jig Saw

22"

45°

Toenail

Brass screws

Support is 18" length of 2"x6"

Toenail

Tub Lids and Seats

A lid for your hot tub is essential; it protects the tub from heat loss, debris, and critters, and, of course, it acts as a safety factor so kids do not fall in. Wood is a good insulator; a ¾-inch-thick tongue-and-groove clear heart redwood lid is very appropriate. You can make a lid (see drawing) or buy one from a supplier. The lid is hinged at the center for easy handling and a lock may be installed on it. Be sure to treat the tub lid with sealants to keep it from warping. Use four or five coats of moisture sealant (at hardware stores); there must be a moisture barrier or the lid will deteriorate.

There is a variety of wooden tub seats; what you choose depends upon your individual needs. Usually two seats are enough in the average 6-foot tub, but you can have as many as six seats if the tub is large enough. These seats are made of 2 x 6-inch planks set on suitable wooden blocks or braces, or of slats on suitable wood supports.

Hooks, Ladders, and Dressing Areas

If you wish to provide hooks and racks for towels or clothes, a railing or other horizontal member of the wooden deck or platform that houses the tub is a convenient location. Each situation has its own answers. Nothing elaborate is necessary; a few wood or brass hooks or towel racks can be placed almost anywhere near the tub.

The free-standing tub requires a ladder so that you can climb in. We recommend the ladders sold by manufacturers of hot tub kits; they are strong, durable, and suited for the tub. You can also buy ladders at

65

lumberyards and secure them in place with wood epoxies (available at hardware stores). Alternately, the bottom of the ladder can be toenailed into the deck and the top of the ladder set against the side of the tub.

Rope ladders are another possibility, although they are more difficult for older people to use. Makeshift steps or sturdy wooden boxes placed in stair-step fashion would also serve the purpose.

Most hot tub areas do not have separate dressing rooms; usually the tub is close to the house so that no additional accommodations are needed. However, if the tub is some distance away, it might be convenient to include a small dressing room or cabana. You can have a carpenter build such a unit, or if you are a good carpenter, do it yourself. Consult the many good books on building outdoor structures.

Sit back, relax, and luxuriate in the swirling waters of your hot tub. A seat is an ideal accessory for comfortable tubbing—add another, and soak with a friend. Photo courtesy Country Comfort Redwood Tubs

This rectangular wooden tub is set on a tiered wooden platform. The hinged lid, which rests, when open, against the backdrop of diagonal pine sheeting, protects the tub from dirt and debris when not in use. Photo courtesy Country Comfort Redwood Tubs

Lighting

In outdoor settings the hot tub is used by devotees at night as well as during the day. Some tubbers say that dusk is the best time to soak—with dinner later. It is a peaceful and even romantic time. But no one wants to be strolling in the garden and plunge into a hot tub unaware—it could be downright dangerous. So if the tub is in the garden or on a deck or patio, there should be some lighting at least for safety purposes, even if you are not romantic or do not use the tub at night.

Standard garden lighting fixtures and setups can be used for hot tub installations. There are special voltage kits, not too expensive, available at lighting suppliers (for garden use) that do the job satisfactorily. Six or eight fixtures strategically placed can add beauty to the area at night and provide safety as well.

If the cost of a lighting system is absolutely beyond your means, consider using a few candles or some kerosene lamps to light the area around the tub when you are using it.

6. Plug into the Sun

Water heating and energy costs are frequent topics of conversation these days and rightly so—energy is becoming scarce and, thus, costly. So what about heating costs for hot tubs? They are much less than you might think, particularly if you use solar energy to heat your hot tub—it works efficiently and cuts fuel bills considerably. Let us look at heating costs both of conventional systems and of solar heating.

Ceramic tiles line the inner rim of this concrete tub and are set at the bottom in a colorful accent. In good weather the sun cooperates to heat the water to the tubber's delight. Photo by Matthew Barr

Water Usage and Heating Costs

Hot tubs hold a great deal of water—as much as 800 gallons—but they are actually water savers. Remember that a standard tub, which holds 35 gallons, drains away the water after one use, whereas in a hot tub the water is recirculated and cleaned for use again and again. You replace the water only once or twice a year, so the water savings are considerable.

You also save money on bathing if you soap up quickly in a shower and rinse off quickly, then soak in your tub to avoid the prolonged running of the shower. In fact, if you hot tub, regular showering can become obsolete.

You may think that it takes a lot of fuel to heat a hot tub, but it does not, because the water is kept warm and in the tub at all times. For example, the average family of four uses 8,000 Btu./day if every member showers daily. However, the average hot tub uses only about 2,000 Btu./day to heat the water, and as many people can use the tub as want to.

Solar Energy

In this day and in days to come we will be looking to the sun for energy—efficient energy at low cost. The concept of a solar heating system for a hot tub is simple. It is based on the principle that hot water rises and cool water falls. As water cools in the tub, the cooler water settles to the bottom. A small pump is used to draw out this water, which is then forced into a header pipe at the bottom of solar collector panels

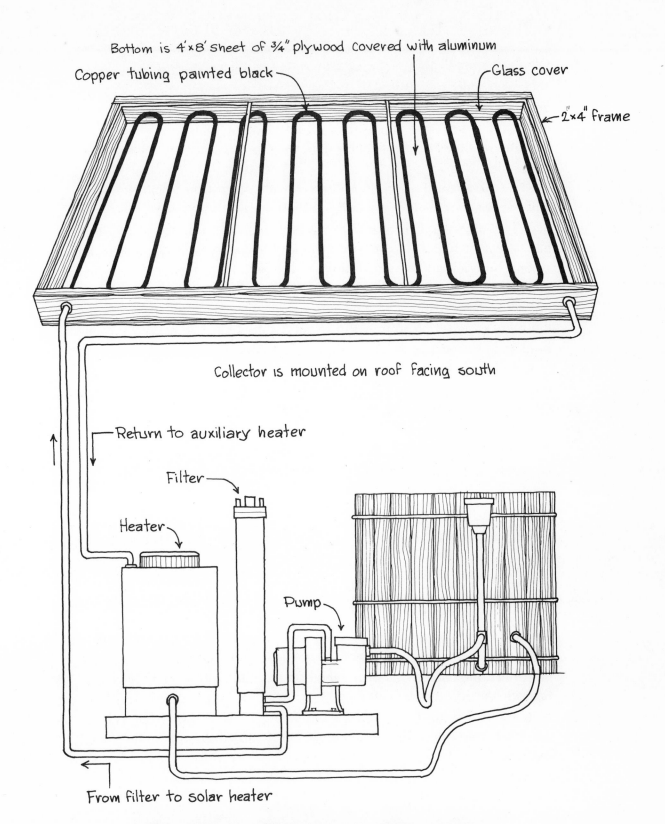

Bottom is 4'×8' sheet of ¾" plywood covered with aluminum

Copper tubing painted black

Glass cover

2"×4" frame

Collector is mounted on roof facing south

Return to auxiliary heater

Filter

Heater

Pump

From filter to solar heater

Solar Water Heater

(of which there are various types—more about them later). Here the water is heated, and as it rises, it recirculates, running through a maze of pipes or water passages to a top header pipe, where it then runs back into the hot tub. No energy is consumed other than that required to operate the small pump, which uses no more energy than a standard light bulb.

This is all well and good when the sun shines, but what happens when it doesn't? Well, most areas of the country have more sunny days than gray days—at least during the tubbing season. And remember that half a loaf of bread is better than none. On a nice sunshiney day the system can increase the water temperature by 5 to 10 degrees. The solar panels can create 1,000 Btu. per square foot. On days that the sun does not shine, an auxiliary heating system will be necessary. (We discuss these in chapter 5.) You may think that it's inefficient to have two types of heating systems, but actually the investment will pay off in the long run. A solar heating system can be operated at minimal cost and will offer you substantial savings in the cost of fuel, even if you do have to run the auxiliary heater at certain times.

Installing a Solar Heater

Perhaps the easiest solar installation for a hot tub is to place the tub at least one foot higher than the top of the solar collectors. In this way no circulating pump is needed; gravity and convection will do the work. Hot water is less dense than cool water so it will rise naturally from the collectors; the cooler water from the bottom of the tub will fall by gravity back down into the collectors. Always insulate supply and return lines and be sure they are pitched so that there are no air locks. Install a check valve in the supply line so that reverse circulation does not occur in cold weather.

This square wooden tub sits on a slatted wooden deck and is partially sheltered by an overhang that extends from the house. A sunny day such as this is ideal for the use of a solar collector. Photo courtesy Country Comfort Redwood Tubs

Solar collectors should face to the south. A float-type air vent is necessary at the highest point of the system so that you can bleed off any air locks that may develop in the lines. The air vent also acts as an automatic air eliminator when water is first put into the system, and as a vacuum breaker to permit drainage of water. To be used as a vacuum breaker a cushion of air must remain inside the air vent; to provide for this cushion, loosen the top cap about two turns.

Not all types of hot tub installations are suitable for the gravity siphon system, but where it is applicable it works well.

Rooftop Solar Heating Systems

The rooftop solar installation is popular and is being installed on many new homes. When used with the hot tub a small 1/20 hp pump is needed to push cooler water from the bottom of the tub up into the collectors. A pair of thermostatic sensors are installed to tell the pump when to work and when not to work. These are tapped into place on the pipes at the hottest and coolest parts of the system. The thermostats are wired into a control box. The box also contains a shut off so that when water in the tub reaches the desired temperature the pump will shut down automatically to prevent overheating.

All parts of the solar heating system should be well insulated to prevent unnecessary heat loss. To determine the size of the collector plate or area you will need, multiply the surface area of the water by three or four. For example, a tub 5 feet in diameter would need from 47 to 63 feet of collector coverage.

Unless you live in a climate that has a stable temperature all year round, the sun will not be enough to heat your tub water. You will still need the support of a gas or electric system—but, of course, with your solar heating unit, you won't have to use it as much.

Solar Collectors

There are so many solar collectors now manufactured that it is difficult to single out any one type. An early version is the mattress type, really a sandwich of flattened polyvinyl chloride tubing with turbulators that tumble the water around. It does not work as well as the newer copper or anodized aluminum panel, which is rigid. The most popular collector consists of copper tubes laid on aluminum fins and covered with glass or Filon (a rigid plastic) to insulate the tubing. Polyethylene tubing is also used in panels because it can take in heat from any angle. The glazed, or glass, collector is most efficient because it takes in radiant heat easily and does not lose it.

Panels come in various sizes and under various brand names; consult your local phone book for manufacturers and distributors. You will find them listed under the SOLAR headings.

7. Where to Put Your Tub

Whether you have a wooden tub or a fiberglass spa, where to put it involves a bit of planning. In this chapter we discuss some design ideas for the location of your hot tub. The following chapter contains specific instructions for building the type of setting you decide on.

OPPOSITE: This is a beautifully appointed tub set in a deck adjacent to the house and surrounded by a platform on one side. A simple set of steps leads to the tub. The area is partially enclosed by a fence, providing a view of the forest beyond. Photo by Matthew Barr

A flagstone and brick patio surrounded by a fence and a low wall is the setting for an octagonal fiberglass tub. It is located on the south side of the house, only 20 feet away. Photo © Riviera Spas. Used with permission

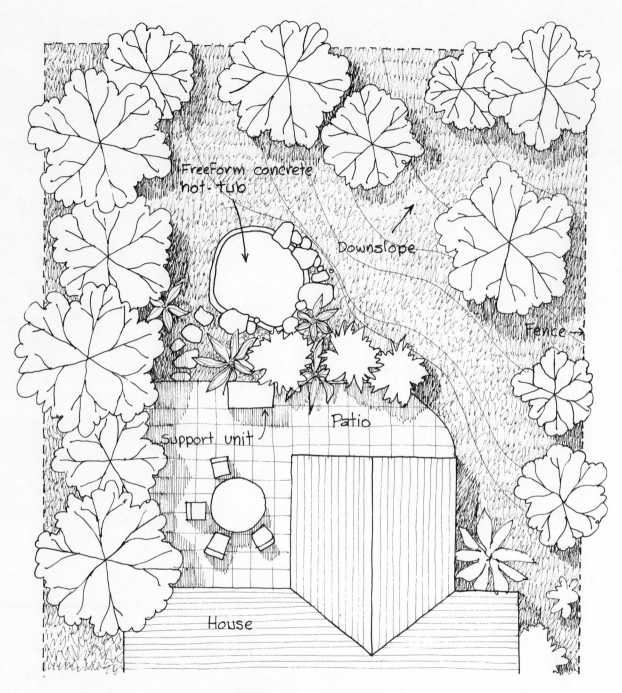

FreeForm concrete hot-tub

Downslope

Fence →

Patio

Support unit

House

Plot Plan

80

Outdoors

In temperate climates most people prefer the tub outdoors, where it can be enjoyed in a natural setting. Gardens and decks are favorite locations and provide opportunities to create a lovely environment. The otherwise empty space of a patio also can be enhanced by the addition of a tub; this location offers special convenience because it is close to the house. The area adjoining a swimming pool is another good place for the hot tub. (In many cases the hot tub, usually a fiber-glass one, has replaced or augmented the swimming pool.)

Most people put their tub at the rear of the house, for privacy. However, space, light, and other considerations may make that undesirable. If so, it is possible to place a hot tub at the side or front of a house; if properly designed and well protected by screens, it will look fine there.

Plot Plan

If you tell someone you are making a plot plan, it sounds very impressive, but actually all you are doing is making a sketch of the area where the tub will be installed—in the garden or on the patio, near the bedroom or the living room. The idea is to place the tub where it will fit in well with your family's activities, and in general where it will look good.

You do not have to be an artist to make a plot plan; all you need is a piece of paper and a pencil. Measure the footage of the patio or garden, then map it out on paper. Put in shapes for trees and other existing shrubbery, other shapes for outbuildings, and, of course, a big box shape for your house.

Once you have it all on paper, sit back and look. What are you looking for? The ideal spot for your tub: where it will be convenient to the house, where it will enjoy sufficient privacy, and where it will be protected from the elements. Make many sketches with the tub in different locations until you come upon the right arrangement. In planning, be sure to take into account existing shrubs and trees and try to build within these limitations—it is easier (and less expensive) to build a deck around a tree or bank of shrubs than to remove them. On the other hand, you may want to add extra shrubbery for further privacy and protection, and a deck or patio if you don't already have one. Remember that it is far easier to play around on paper like this than to build a tub and landscape it, only to decide that the location is inconvenient and have to change it.

Deck, Patio, or Garden

In California the deck is an extension of a house, and it is a favorite place for a hot tub. The wooden hot tub looks good in or on a deck; it can be set flush into the deck, be a free-standing tub with a ladder, or be partially sunken. Installing the hot tub in a deck is not difficult, requiring 3 x 6 redwood joists on piers or a 4-inch-thick concrete pad, as described in chapter 3. The joists are placed between the tub and the concrete. Provide a slight slope for runoff on the concrete slab. The joists bear the weight of the tub and provide the necessary air ventilation between the tub and slab.

Some people sink a wood tub into the ground, but this may create drainage problems and cause the hole to cave in. Remember that soil and water contact will rot wooden tubs, unless a gravel backfill to absorb moisture is included. The partially sunken tub or the flush tub are perhaps the most handsome; to my eye the free-standing tub looks somewhat ungainly.

A garden location was chosen for a round fiberglass tub sunk into a small brick patio. Soaking in a setting landscaped as beautifully as this is a tubber's delight. Photo courtesy Avalon Spas

This wooden tub is nestled into the corner of a deck, protected on all sides by walls of pine boards arranged in a diagonal pattern. Hanging ferns add a lovely note of color to the scene. Photo courtesy Country Comfort Redwood Tubs

Do not place your tub directly on a deck even if the deck has suitable supports such as beams and rafters. If you do, you may find that your upright tub will become a sunken tub, to your dismay. The tub must rest on a basic foundation, as previously described. When building a deck, leave an opening for the hot tub and, if necessary, openings for any trees in the deck area.

Another favorite place for a fiberglass or concrete hot tub is a terrace or patio. Installing a sunken tub in this location requires work, but it is worth the effort. First, the hole must be dug, which can be a tedious and demanding job (hauling soil is no joke), and then the hole must be properly prepared for the tub. The installation here is similar to that for a swimming pool: suitable facings to hold the earth in place and concrete coatings. (Follow the directions as in chapter 3 for concrete tubs.) This is not an impossible job nor exorbitant in cost—it just requires some doing.

The garden is another place for the tub, and if the garden is near a bedroom or bath, the tub works beautifully, providing easy access to changing areas, fresh towels, and so forth. Installation of a tub in a garden is similar to that on a patio or terrace.

Indoors

An indoor hot tub provides a beautiful way to bathe year-round in privacy and in all types of weather. It can be of either wood or fiberglass. Fiberglass tubs—often called spas—come in many shapes and styles. Some are made to fit in a corner; others are round or amoeba-shaped and create a stunning accent when placed in the center of a room. Indoor installation is somewhat more costly than outdoor installation. But the advantage, in addition to year-round use, is that the indoor hot tub can totally replace your old-fashioned bathtub; with hydrojets, it provides a beautiful way to relax and rejuvenate body and soul.

One of the most handsome hot tub installations I have seen was in a greenhouse. The lushness of the natural surroundings created a heavenly environment for a hot soaking—if you could not forget your worries here, you could not forget them any place. Soaking in a hot tub in a greenhouse filled with plants is an experience akin to returning to the womb.

Not all of us have such an ideal situation for the tub—most indoor tubs are in conventional places, such as the bathroom, where plumbing is already available. Yet it is easy to make this room more inviting; just a few colorful plants will help provide the ambience you are seeking.

The indoor hot tub provides the same benefits as the outdoor hot tub: steaming water, hydrojets, and the pleasure of relaxing while cleansing your body, with the added advantage of year-round availability.

This sunken fiberglass tub is situated in a bedroom, but the handsome rock wall behind it creates the illusion of a natural outdoor setting. The corner arrangement is a convenient location for the bedroom tub. Photo by Matthew Barr

Indoor Greenery

By all means, whether indoors or out, embellish the area around the tub with plants. Indoors, you can create a lush tropical atmosphere by using certain plants; in bathrooms or areas where there is water, the plants will benefit from the extra humidity.

For indoor greenery around a hot tub, consider the popular houseplants, such as philodendron, ferns, and palms. These are appropriate for the tub scene and can be arranged in decorative containers near the hot tub. The best way to arrange plants is to place several pots at one end of the tub in a handsome grouping. Ferns are especially attractive near water. None of these plants needs bright or direct light—they will get along beautifully with only moderate or indirect light.

For another effect, use one large specimen plant, such as a *Ficus Benjamina,* in a decorative container; set seasonal flowering plants around the accent tree. For other plants that you might use indoors to accent your hot tub, see the accompanying chart. For further variety, spend some time browsing among the mail-order suppliers, which you can find listed in the classified section of any garden magazine.

INDOOR GREENERY FOR THE HOT TUB

ANTHURIUMS: Lovely 20-inch plants with lush green leaves—they love humidity and need only indirect sunlight.

CHLOROPHYTUM: Also called spider plants. These popular hanging plants with long grassy leaves and even longer baby "spiders" grow easily and tolerate low light. They look lovely on small stands near the tub.

ORCHIDS: Surprisingly, these plants are easy to grow. They are extremely handsome near the water. The flowers are exotic and come in a wide variety of colors. They require indirect but bright light.

BROMELIADS: Almost perfect houseplants because they require so little care. They fare best with bright light (sunlight if possible) and should be kept moderately moist at all times. Some varieties in this family, which is characterized by rosette or vase-shaped leaves, are Aechmeas, Guzmanias, Billbergias, and Vriesias.

Landscaping for the Hot Tub

If you are going to have the comfort and luxury (with minimal cost) of a hot tub, you should have the tub located properly to benefit from nature's greenery. If you place your tub in the right location outdoors, you will be able to use it more months of the year. So, positioning the tub is important. (Remember the plot plan mentioned earlier.)

In most cases you are going to want privacy when you tub whether you are modest or not. And the most privacy is usually found in the rear of the house, so this is probably where the tub will go. Exactly where is the question.

Put your tub where there is protection from the wind and from storms—although many people delight in soaking in a hot tub in cold weather or a rainstorm. These are the stalwart ones; most people will elect to be inside at such times. However, landscaping will offer some protection from the elements.

Don't let the word *landscaping* scare you. It need not be either complicated or expensive. It merely means putting the tub where there are some natural barriers such as shrubs and trees to protect it from harsh northwest winds. If there are no existing shrubs, plant some. Trees and shrubs grow up before you know it and will offer a suitable barrier in a few years. In fact, if you buy your plants in 5-gallon cans you probably won't have to wait for them to grow to provide cover—they will be tall enough to offer sufficient screening from neighbors' view. Most trees and shrubs are available from nurseries in either 1-gallon or 5-gallon cans. This is one time it pays to get the biggest.

The best protection against wind in the outdoor garden area is three rows of trees or shrubs. Plant the shrubs in an arc at the northwest side; space them four feet apart—three good shrubs will do it. In back of these, plant another row and finally in back of these, some trees—one or two will do fine. In short terms you get maximum protection from wind and cold with a three-row setup. Cost? About $100 for plant material

Another view of the corner fiberglass tub showing its placement in the bedroom. Indoor-outdoor carpeting is a practical floor covering for the indoor setting. Photo by Matthew Barr

and well worth it because with nature's help you can sit in your tub until November (in most parts of the country) without discomfort. Without the ideal green setup you might want to scurry in after Labor Day. With it, you can get out and tub as early as late March (in most climates).

While you're waiting for the trees and shrubs to grow, or if you'd rather not plant them, consider using vines. They grow much faster and make excellent background plantings, either in the ground or in containers. See chapter 8 for instructions on building a trellis to support them.

Another alternative is to build a fence, though this does not buffer the wind as effectively as greenery. Wind will generally roll over a fence and pour into the tub area in a cold wave. An exception is the properly engineered fence of louvers; it is expensive, but it will protect the tub area from wind.

Trees and Shrubs

When you are landscaping with trees, it is best to avoid the deciduous ones, which drop their leaves and seedpods. Not only do the falling leaves reduce privacy and insulation against wind, they also can create a constant cleaning problem in the hot tub. To avoid this, use evergreen trees that will be handsome all year long and create a minimum of debris. In addition to the privacy and wind protection provided by trees, they also are just plain pretty to look at when you soak in your tub and help to put you in total touch with nature.

Shrubs too have their many uses as backgrounds for tubs. Here again, select shrubs that will not require frequent cleaning up.

The accompanying chart provides some general suggestions for suitable trees and shrubs—enough to get you started. There are, of course, many other varieties you can use. If you're feeling adventurous, take the time to visit a large nursery in your locale, check out the stock, and talk with the dealer. But remember: don't buy too much on your first visit. It's better to purchase a few plants at the beginning and add to them later as necessary. Overcrowding plants to begin with will stunt their growth eventually; not only will this mean wasted effort and expense, but it will inhibit your desired goal of greenery as a natural screen. So go lightly to start with.

TREES

CHAMAECYPARIS: A large group of evergreens commonly known as cypress or cedar; they grow to about 20 feet. Many varieties.

JUNIPERUS: Another large group of needle-type trees, commonly called juniper, that make handsome privacy hedges; grow to about 20 feet but can be trimmed to about 8 feet.

TAXUS: Known commonly as yews, these include some of our best hedge plants; they grow to about 20 feet but can be trimmed to 6 or 8 feet.

SHRUBS

BUXUS: Known commonly as boxwood, this group contains many varieties of evergreen plants that make suitable 6-foot barriers.

ILEX: Commonly called hollies, growing to about 8 feet. Variegated leaves, evergreen. Slow-growing.

TAXUS: Yew type shrubs growing to only 5 feet and ideal for trimming and shaping. Dark green accent.

BERBERIS: The common barberries, with several varieties, growing to about 5 feet. Deciduous.

COTONEASTER, LIGUSTRUM, PHILADELPHUS, SPIRAEA, and *VIBURNUM* are other deciduous shrubs for decorating hot tub areas.

Vines

If you want beauty and rapid growth at the same time, consider planting some vines. Most of them grow tall in one season and offer the additional advantage of flowers—incredibly beautiful flowers. Lovely clematis and bougainvillaea are enchanting and bloom on and off all summer long. They make a tub party colorful and are choice plants to make the outdoor area attractive. Consult the chart for some suggested varieties.

VINES

BOUGAINVILLAEA: A showy evergreen vine for temperate climates with handsome red or orange flowers. Beautiful on trellis.

BIGNONIA: Called the trumpet vine, this handsome flowering plant has orange blossoms, grows fast, and provides a heavy screening. (Also called Clystoma.)

CLEMATIS: Clematis are among the most decorative and beautiful of all vines. A favorite is Clematis armandii, the lovely white flowering species. Evergreen, with lush growth.

JASMINUM: Called jasmine and known for scent; dozens of varieties; choose what is available in your area. Very pretty.

ENGLISH IVY: Rapid growing. Many varieties.

8.
Decks, Platforms, Patios, Screens, Indoor Installations
—and How to Build Them

In the preceding chapter we discussed the various factors to consider in choosing a location for your hot tub and designing the area around it. In this chapter we will show you how to construct specific types of installations.

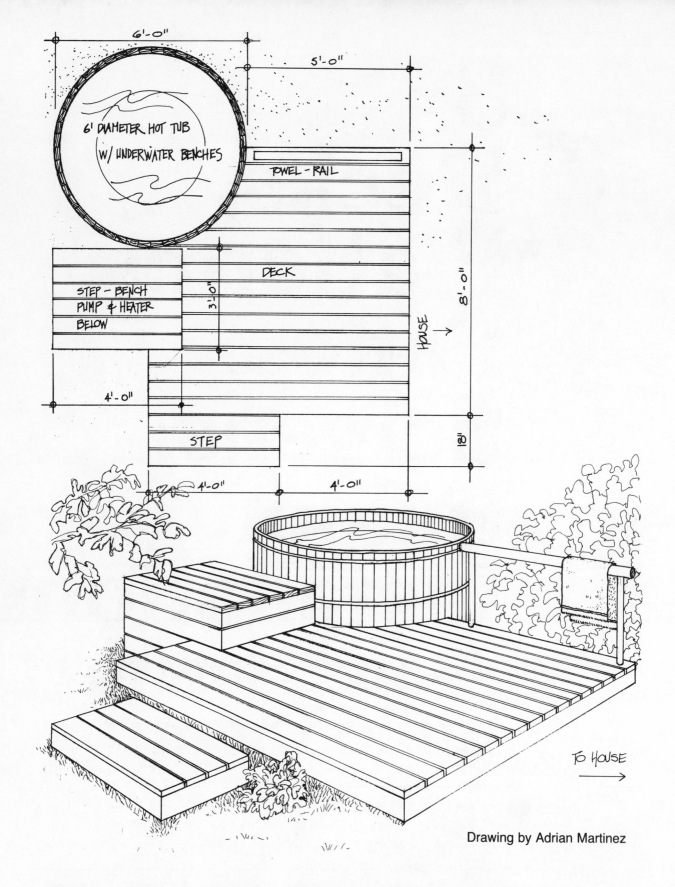

6'-0"
5'-0"

6' DIAMETER HOT TUB
W/ UNDERWATER BENCHES

TOWEL - RAIL

DECK

STEP - BENCH
PUMP & HEATER
BELOW

3'-0"

8'-0"

HOUSE →

4'-0"

18"

STEP

4'-0"

4'-0"

TO HOUSE →

Drawing by Adrian Martinez

The Hot Tub Environment

The Deck

A deck around a hot tub provides safe and easy access to the tub. In addition, as an extension of the house, it creates a unified design for the tub area, enhances the appearance (and property value) of the house, and provides attractive space for relaxing after tubbing. You need not be an expert carpenter to build a deck; all you need is time and some general knowledge of wood. Of course, you can hire someone to build the decking for you—either a hot tub manufacturer or a carpenter—but it will entail some expense. Although concrete decks are often built, here we will discuss only wood decks.

Building codes for decks vary from county to county, so check your local building office before you begin. The planning and construction given here are general and do not necessarily meet legal requirements. Be sure to sketch the layout and plan your requirements carefully before you buy the lumber and start to build; it will save time and money later on.

The typical construction of a deck consists of a foundation, a framework, and a surface. (See drawings for construction details.) Redwood is the material most often used because it resists deterioration from moisture better than other woods and over a period of time weathers into a beautiful color.

A foundation for a low-level deck can be built of 4 x 8-inch posts set on precast concrete piers embedded in concrete footings. The footings anchor the deck to the site and keep the wood from coming in contact with the soil. Footings must extend below the frost line or else water in the concrete will crack the footing when it freezes. Check with your local building office to find out the frost line in your area. Depending upon where you live, you can buy precast footings from suppliers, or use concrete blocks for small ground-level decks. Precast concrete piers are sunk in the concrete footings and must be placed absolutely level so there will be no tilt to the structure. Ideally, the deck should be almost level with the house floor. For a hillside deck, footings must extend at least 30 inches below soil line and be 1 foot or more across.

To build a deck, measure and then outline the area with string and stakes. Locate the position of the corner post and put a stake in place;

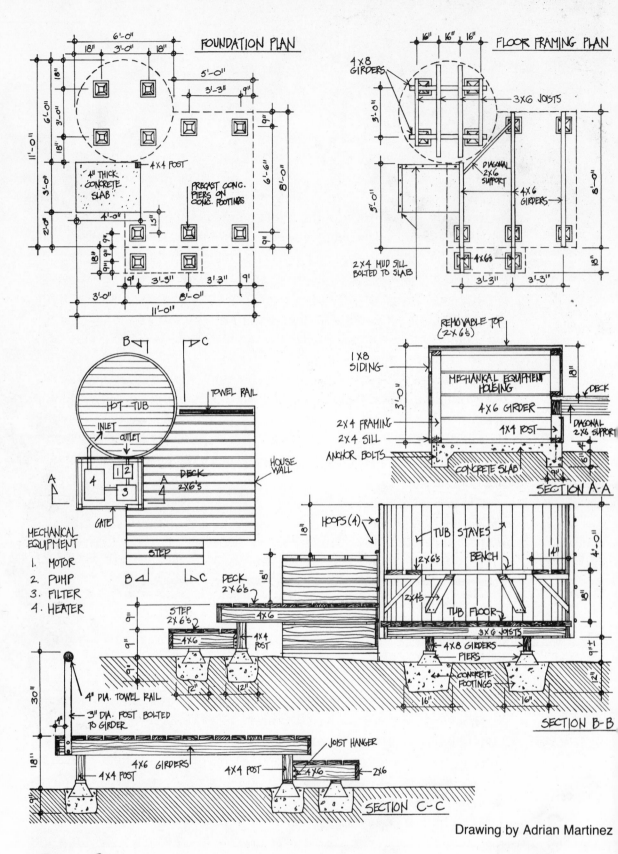

FOUNDATION PLAN

FLOOR FRAMING PLAN

4" THICK CONCRETE SLAB

4X4 POST

PRECAST CONC. PIERS ON CONC. FOOTINGS

4X8 GIRDERS

3X6 JOISTS

DIAGONAL 2X6 SUPPORT

4X6 GIRDERS

2X4 MUD SILL BOLTED TO SLAB

4X6'S

TOWEL RAIL

HOT-TUB

INLET

OUTLET

HOUSE WALL

DECK 2X6'S

GATE

MECHANICAL EQUIPMENT
1. MOTOR
2. PUMP
3. FILTER
4. HEATER

STEP

REMOVABLE TOP (2X6's)

1X8 SIDING

MECHANICAL EQUIPMENT HOUSING

4X6 GIRDER

1X4 POST

DECK

DIAGONAL 2X6 SUPPORT

2X4 FRAMING

2X4 SILL

ANCHOR BOLTS

CONCRETE SLAB

SECTION A-A

HOOPS (4)

TUB STAVES

BENCH

2X6'S

12X6'S

2X4'S

TUB FLOOR

DECK 2X6'S

STEP 2X6'S

4X6

4X4 POST

3X6 JOISTS

4X8 GIRDERS

PIERS

CONCRETE FOOTINGS

SECTION B-B

4" DIA. TOWEL RAIL

3" DIA. POST BOLTED TO GIRDER

4X6 GIRDERS

4X4 POST

JOIST HANGER

4X6

2X6

4X4 POST

SECTION C-C

Drawing by Adrian Martinez

deck construction details

A solid wall of redwood planks makes a handsome backdrop for a hot tub, offering both privacy and protection from wind. One side of the redwood deck is left unscreened so that tubbers can enjoy a view of the woods beyond. Photo by Matthew Barr

Swirling, bubbling water invites bathers into a hot tub that is slightly raised above the decking. The boards of the deck are set at angles to create a pattern, and a portion of the patio beyond is laid with tile. Photo by Matthew Barr

A rectangular hot tub, recessed in an unscreened deck, has a wide rim to provide seating space. The simplicity of the setting is complemented by the spectacular view of the surrounding landscape. Photo courtesy Country Comfort Redwood Tubs

This hot tub was built from a kit, with a row of tiles added as decorative trim. The deck has been designed on several levels, creating steps and a ledge for towels. The trellis behind is set on a curve to echo the shape of the tub. Photo by John Werner

The setting for this handmade rectangular tub has been designed with the utmost simplicity: a frame of steps surrounded by a wall of diagonal pine sheeting. The tub is covered with an ingenious hinged lid. Photo courtesy Country Comfort Redwood Tubs

The spa on the patio is a visual treat as well as a bathing pleasure. Here, an oval tub is set in a border of weathered bricks; the interior is lined with patterned ceramic tile. A stone bench adds charm to the garden setting. Photo courtesy Avalon Spas

Climb up, soak in. This free-standing hot tub, imaginatively screened by a greenhouse partition, has steps with a safety railing and a hinged lid to conserve heat. The auxiliary equipment is hidden in the cabinet at left, which serves as a shelf for potted plants. Photo by Matthew Barr

Another view of the hot tub handsomely set in a patio paved with brick. The tub, or spa, is conveniently located near the house and affords an expansive view of the surrounding garden. Photo by Matthew Barr

An unusual arrangement features a free-standing hot tub on a wood deck, with a sweeping view of the bay—a natural place for soaking. Suitable hedges afford some privacy, and a hinged lid protects the tub when it is not in use. Photo by John Werner

Set on a small wooden deck, this hot tub has been placed directly adjacent to the house. Steps provide access to the tub and the partial surrounding platform, which holds flowering plants.
Photo by Matthew Barr

Indoor tubs are a luxury because they allow you to soak at any time of year and in all kinds of weather. The tile flooring used here is both practical and attractive. A special enclosure was built for this tub to keep water away from the rest of the house; it adds to the intimacy of the setting. Photo courtesy Avalon Spas

The corner location of this rectangular tub creates a cozy environment for a trio of happy tubbers. Although the tub is situated indoors, the clever addition of a skylight allows natural light to illuminate the room. The tub could easily accommodate twice as many tubbers. Photo courtesy Country Comfort Redwood Tubs

A conventional round wooden tub, sunk into a corner of a deck, is surrounded by a ledge that creates an attractive niche. Fencing has been installed to ensure privacy, and seasonal potted plants have been added for color. Photo by Matthew Barr

then run a nylon string line to the next post hole location. Put in a stake; continue until all corners have stakes. Once you have located the post holes, excavate them with a post hole digger or shovel; lay a bed of concrete in each hole and set on that the precast piers.

The 4 x 6- or 4 x 8-inch post is the most used support for ground-level decks; it bears a weight of 8,000 pounds up to a height of 8 feet. For hillside construction where there are heavier loads, you will need substantially heavier posts: 6 x 6s or perhaps even 8 x 8s. (Local building departments can advise you, or your lumber house can supply this information.)

Beams can be toenailed to posts or nailed with strap metal that comes in L- or T-shaped or straight pieces. Joists that will run lengthwise can be nailed on top of the beams or attached flush with their tops.

Here is a summary of the typical procedure for building a deck for a hot tub:

1. Establish the location of the concrete footings for both deck and hot tub.
2. Dig footing holes to their proper depths and locate the marker lines.
3. Pour concrete in the holes. Place the pier forms in position, leveling them with each other with a line level.
4. Establish the desired level of the deck and measure down the depth of the decking plus the joists. Mark the ledger (horizontal board) and secure it to the stud, starting at the center.
5. After determining the heights, set the posts and check for plumb, using a carpenter's level on two sides.
6. With a piece of scrap lumber set on the posts, check to make sure all the parts in the row are on an even plane.
7. With a measuring tape or string, check the level between the ledger and the beam to see that they are flush.
8. Secure the joist hanger to the post.
9. Place the beam on the post and toenail it in place.
10. Use the house wall as the base point to ensure that decking will be true. Be sure the first deck board is a straight line.
11. Nail the boards in place, using a ½-inch to ¾-inch spacer (a block of wood) between each board to guarantee even spaces.
12. To install tub, cut out appropriate hole in deck, and then either install flush or sunken. If the tub is to be a free-standing one, it will still need a separate foundation as explained earlier.

This hot tub, built from a kit, is beautifully situated on a wooden platform at some distance from the house. The wide sill around the tub is ideal for holding towels and potted plants. Photo by Matthew Barr

The Platform

If your house has no space for a deck, the area around your house does not lend itself to a deck, or you simply do not like decks, you can surround your hot tub with a separate elevated platform—somewhat like an oasis—in the garden or near the house. The platform is a simple wood structure using 2 x 6-inch boards set on precast concrete piers sunk in the ground. See the drawing for a sample plan of a platform surrounding a 6-foot-diameter hot tub. You will need to add steps to provide access to the tub; you can make them from 2 x 12-inch boards for the framework and 2 x 6-inch boards used for steps.

The Patio

A patio is a hard-surface pad of a certain size, usually adjoining the house. Whether it is of concrete or paved with bricks, it can be a barren expanse if not handled properly. If it contains a hot tub recessed into the ground, it can produce a very dramatic effect.

Suitable materials for outdoor floors include brick, tile, concrete, paving blocks, fieldstone, and flagstone. Other materials, such as gravel chips, fir bark, cinders, plastic stones, lava rock, dolomite, and crushed brick, are less durable and may have to be replaced yearly, as does indoor-outdoor carpeting, which now comes in many colors and designs in easy-to-install squares.

Because there are so many outdoor floor materials, select one that is durable and in character with the house. A floor that is not comfortable to walk on with bare feet, such as gravel, or one that needs constant cleaning (textured concrete, for example) is a bad choice. And when selecting the patio floor, do consider the cost and installation fees.

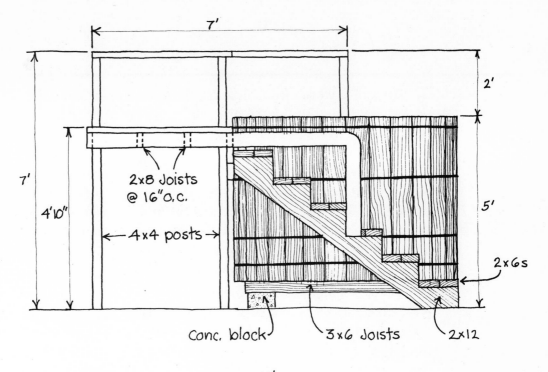

7'

2'

7'

4'10"

5'

2x8 Joists
@ 16"O.C.

4x4 posts

2x6s

Conc. block

3x6 Joists

2x12

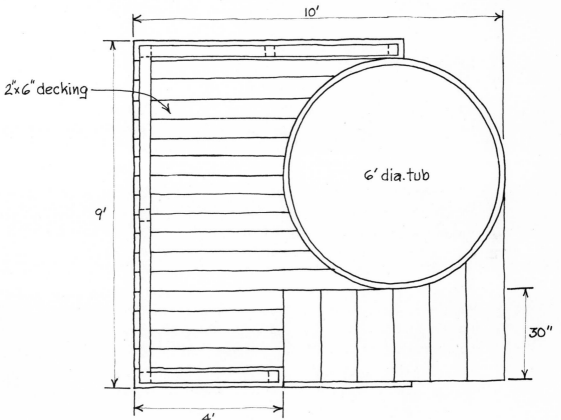

10'

2"x6"decking

9'

6' dia.tub

4'

30"

Tub on Platform

The following information on paving materials includes the most popular and how to use them. It also touches on the less popular but equally attractive flagstone, fieldstone, slate, and all-weather carpeting.

CONCRETE Concrete may not be as handsome as some other pavings, but it is durable and fairly inexpensive. It is easy to clean and can be installed by a paving contractor in a few hours. If you object to the cold feeling of concrete, mix it with a color, paint it, or dye the top layer with liquid. The surface can be finished in a variety of textures, from smooth to rough.

An aggregate floor is another idea. This is a floor made of concrete with small stones on its surface. The textured finish is handsome and blends with plantings and lawns. The uneven texture breaks the monotony of a large area of paving, especially when the aggregate surface has a wood grid pattern. The pebbly surface of aggregate concrete also eliminates glare and guarantees sure traction if water collects on it. And when this paving collects dirt—as it will—it is easy to hose clean.

The construction of a masonry patio is, of course, more complicated and more costly than deck building, but it can be done. The hard part is digging out the site. Working with concrete is not difficult, but it is not a simple matter and requires some know-how. Although you can install a small area of concrete yourself, it is best to hire a professional for the larger job. However, you can save part of the cost of the floor by having the area ready for the installer. For a tub 5 feet in diameter, a patio 12 x 20 feet would be a good size. Outline these dimensions by setting out 2 x 2-inch stakes with string stretched between them. Dig out 2 to 4 inches and remove all trash from the soil. Set permanent or temporary header boards (boards on edge) in place, being sure the top surface is flush with the grade you want for the concrete. Drive additional 2 x 2-inch stakes at 2-foot intervals along each side of the patio, lining them up carefully with the guide string. Nail 10-inch-wide strips of ¼-inch plywood to the insides of the stakes, to act as forms for the concrete. Forms can be brushed with soil to make them easier to remove after the concrete is poured and set.

Wet the soil a few times the day before the concrete is to be poured. The night before, wet it again so it will be damp when the concrete is

A sunken fiberglass tub is set flush in a fieldstone patio, in close proximity to the house. The greenery in the garden is lush and varied, with tall plants in the rear to create a sense of privacy. Photo © Riviera Spas. Used with permission

poured. Soil that is dry absorbs moisture from the concrete and weakens it.

To build a small patio yourself, rent a portable mixer—ask for a half-bag machine—revolved by a gasoline motor. You will need 16 yards of cement to build a 12 x 16-foot patio 2 inches thick. Using the proportions of 1 cubic foot of sand to ½ sack of cement, place the materials in the revolving drum and let them mix. Then add 1 cubic foot of gravel, and let the mixture tumble for about 4 minutes. Pour the mixture into a wheelbarrow (rent one from a hardware store), and dump the mixture into the forms. Make pavings 3 to 4 inches thick. Smooth out the wet concrete with a wood float tool.

Different finishes can be applied for variation. Make a slick, or hard, finish by moving a steel trowel over the surface when it is partially hardened. Do the first troweling lightly, just enough to smooth the texture. Then trowel again with more pressure. This floor is somewhat uninteresting.

Use a mason's wood trowel (float) to make the floor smooth but not shiny. For an interesting surface, brush the slightly hardened concrete with a broom—more difficult to clean but handsome.

TILE The color of tiles harmonizes well with plants. Tile is smoother than brick, easier to clean, and has a lovely finished look when properly installed. If the patio floor extends into the house, tile is always the decorator's choice.

Outdoor tile is almost always rough-surfaced and usually ¾ or ⅞ inch thick. Quarry tile makes the best patio floor; it is a heavy-duty ceramic material that comes in square, rectangular, or odd shapes. The standard sizes are 3 x 3 to 9 x 9 inches. Some tiles have lightly textured surfaces; others have fired-in designs. They come in a wide range of colors, with brown or red hues the most popular.

Most but not all tiles need a mortar bed to prevent their cracking. It is best to have a professional do this work.

If the soil is flat and stable and you want to try to lay tile on a bed of sand and earth, by all means do so, using the following process. Dig out the soil to about 1 inch below the desired grade and tamp down the earth with a board. Put the outer border in place—rows of tile or header boards—and allow a drainage slope of ⅛ inch per foot. Install a ½-inch bed of sand, and level it with a board. Do *not* use more than a ½-inch bed of sand, or the tiles may tilt when you step on them. Set the tiles in place, starting in a corner, and butt them tightly against each other. Tap each one with a wooden block to bed it firmly into the sand. Cut last tiles if necessary with a tile cutter.

A Riviera spa with hydrojets (note foaming water) is placed in the garden on a concrete-and-brick patio adjoining the house. This is an idyllic situation for a tub, complete with fencing for privacy. Photo © Riviera Spas. Used with permission

BRICK   Brick is a popular paving because it is handsome, easy to install, and lasts a long time. You can set brick in mortar, or use the simple method of brick-on-sand. This latter method allows for mistakes; it is easy to take up sections and relay them.

Brick comes in a variety of earthy colors, in rough and smooth surfaces, glazed or unglazed. There are many shapes, including hexagon, octagon, and fleur-de-lis. And colored brick—green, blue, olive—is now also offered.

Generally, try to use hard-burned rather than "green" brick for outdoors. It should be dark red rather than salmon in color, which indicates an underburned process and thus less durability. When you decide on the kind of brick, be sure the dealer has a sufficient quantity to complete the area. There is usually some dimensional variation and color difference among different batches of bricks, so to keep the surface uniform try to purchase all the brick you will need at one time.

If you are in a climate where winters are severe, buy SW (severe weathering) brick. It is easy to install a brick-on-sand paving if you do it in sections—a small piece at a time—rather than trying to finish an entire floor in a day.

Brick can be laid in an incredible number of patterns: herringbone or basketweave, for example. The herringbone pattern is handsome for large areas; use basketweave for smaller ones. You can also combine brick with other materials—squares of grass or cinders—in endless designs, such as a grid pattern alternating with redwood.

To cut or trim bricks, cut a groove along one side of the brick with a cold chisel and then give it a sharp severing blow. Smooth uneven bricks by rubbing the edges with another brick.

To install brick on sand, excavate the plot to 4 inches; level the soil with a board and tamp it down thoroughly. Remove lumpy clay and debris. Slope the floor away from the house—1 inch for every 6 feet of paving—to provide drainage. Put in a 2- to 3-inch bed of absolutely level sand. Set the bricks as close together as possible, and check each row with a level as you go. Then dust sand into the cracks.

For edgings, use 2 x 4-inch wooden header strips held firmly in place with 2 x 2-inch stakes, or set a border of bricks in concrete. Brick can also be set in mortar, but this is usually a job for a professional bricklayer.

A handsome platform seating area adjoins a wooden tub built from a kit. The tub sits on a deck with suitable supports below. A handsome diamond-pattern trellis screen complements the picture; small vines and staghorn ferns are used for accent. Photo by Matthew Barr

Trellises

A lattice or trellis structure adds charm to the tubbing area and is a handsome way to ensure privacy. A trellis is not difficult to make. Basically, it is a grid pattern made of lathing. Laths are about ⅜ inch thick and 1⅝ inches wide; they are sold in lengths of 6, 8, and 10 feet in bundles of 50 pieces. There are two grades of lath milled, one with blemishes and knotholes, and the other—called surfaced lath—almost (but not totally) free of defects. This second type is preferable.

The standard lath that comes in bundles is usually redwood or red cedar. Both are excellent woods for outdoors because they contain decay-resistant oil and weather beautifully. If you cannot get these woods, use pine or fir, but apply a protective coating (paint, stain, sealer, or wax) to protect them from weather.

To make the trellis, first construct a frame for it. Use 4 x 4-inch posts for vertical supports. Sink them into the ground about 18 inches deep and anchor them in a bed of cement; be sure they are absolutely level. For horizontal framing at top and bottom of trellis use 2 x 4-inch lumber.

To make the grid pattern, start with a piece of lath at one end of the frame, laid either horizontally, vertically, or diagonally; nail both ends to the frame. Lay the next piece of lath parallel to this and continue working until the entire frame is covered. Space laths about 1 inch apart using a 1-inch block or piece of lath as a spacer to keep the spaces even. Lay the remaining laths perpendicular to this foundation, also spaced 1 inch apart. Spacing for the grid pattern is generally 1 inch; use a 1-inch block as a "spacer" as you nail laths in place. The open work pattern allows air to circulate but provides some privacy; if you want more privacy, space the laths closer together.

If the span of the trellis is more than 6 feet install a brace—a 2 x 6-inch board in the center of the trellis running vertically.

The Hot Tub Indoors

If you are thinking of remodeling your bathroom, why not consider enlarging it a bit and adding a hot tub? Indoor hot tubs are gaining in popularity; in addition to their psychological and physical benefits, they add value and beauty to the conventional bathroom. If your bathroom is

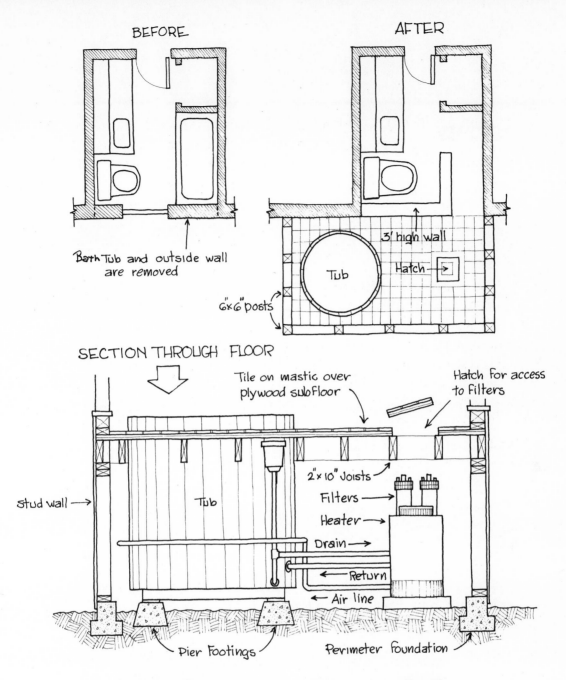

BEFORE

AFTER

Bath Tub and outside wall are removed

3' high wall

Tub

Hatch

6"x6" posts

SECTION THROUGH FLOOR

Tile on mastic over plywood subfloor

Hatch for access to filters

2"x10" Joists

Filters

Heater

Drain

Return

Air line

Stud wall

Tub

Pier Footings

Perimeter foundation

Bathroom Remodel

on the ground floor, you can enlarge it by knocking out the exterior wall and building on an addition; this is not a difficult job and generally can be handled by a good home carpenter. Wing walls are added after existing walls are removed and then a new wall put in place using standard stud and frame construction. Roofing and flooring complete the picture. (For further details, consult a book on bathroom remodeling.)

Bathroom Remodel

PERSPECTIVE

The drawings here illustrate one way to make a bathroom larger and add a wooden hot tub at the same time.

Installing a fiberglass hot tub indoors is similar to installing a bathtub. The opening must be framed and plumbed to accept the tub, and there must be suitable plumbing connections. These operations are best performed by a carpenter and a plumber. Note that unlike the bathtub, which is usually placed against a wall and framed in an

Indoor Tile Spa

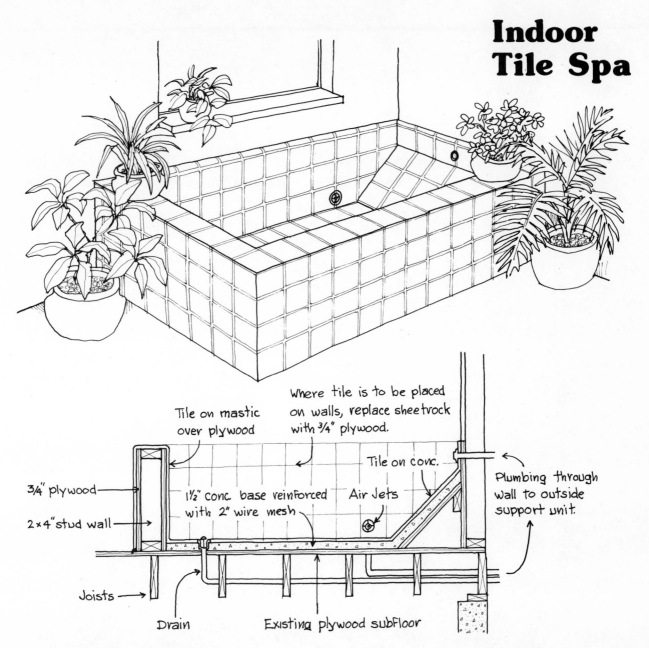

Tile on mastic over plywood

Where tile is to be placed on walls, replace sheetrock with ¾" plywood.

Tile on conc.

Plumbing through wall to outside support unit.

¾" plywood

2×4" stud wall

1½" conc. base reinforced with 2" wire mesh

Air Jets

Joists

Drain

Existing plywood subfloor

opening, the hot tub or spa can also be placed in the center of the bathroom, where it serves as stunning accent.

While the bathroom is a convenient room in which to install a hot tub—since the plumbing is already in place—many people opt to put it in the bedroom. This will obviously be more costly and complicated, since the plumbing will have to be extended some distance. However, the arrangement enables you to enjoy the wonderful luxury of hopping

right into bed after a nice hot soak. There is little else so conducive to a restful, refreshing sleep—and it is probably a good antidote to insomnia. In practical terms, too, the addition of the hot tub to the bedroom adds value to the home.

The first thing to consider is whether the floor will hold the weight of a hot tub. Most houses are built with framing adequate to carry such weight, but since each house is built a little differently, it would be wise to check this out with a contractor or someone who knows about construction. (The same construction precautions that apply to water beds should be followed here.)

Whether you install the tub in the bathroom or the bedroom, it is best to have the plumbing done by a professional. Although it is costly, few people are familiar enough with pipes and sockets to do the job right.

The sunken spa set in a corner of the room is a convenient design for a bedroom. It makes plumbing connections easier to install and keeps the tub out of the way of other activities. Set the tub away from the bed and furnishings to protect them from getting wet, and surround it with indoor-outdoor or bathroom carpeting to absorb water. Ensure adequate ventilation—windows, doors, or small exhaust fans—to help keep the room free of excess moisture.

Some people find the noise of the bubbling water at night a soothing inducement to sleep; it's like camping out near a running brook. However, if the noise bothers you, you can always turn off the jets when you're ready to go to bed.

Enclosures

If you live in a region where the weather is very cold or rainy at certain times of the year, and you still want to put your hot tub in the garden, all is not lost! Why not try enclosing your tub in a structure all its

OPPOSITE: An interior setting was chosen for this kit wooden tub. It is sheltered by its own structure (complete with skylight) adjacent to the house and the garden. Photo by Matthew Barr

A deep round tub is partially surrounded by a wooden structure that attractively conceals the tub's mechanisms and provides ample surface area for supplies. The tub is easily reached by ascending a small ladder. Photo by Matthew Barr

own, such as a greenhouse or a small dome. You may have such a small building already on your property, in which case it will be a simple matter to add a tub. The advantage of enclosing a hot tub is immediately seen: You can soak in it year round. A hot soak is far more invigorating on a cold night than on a warm one, and there is something very rewarding about tubbing indoors in soothing heat while outdoors the snow flies. If the structure is not too large, the steam from the tub will be sufficient to heat the space. A thick towel and a warm robe and slippers for the trip back to the house will be enough to keep you from feeling like a polar bear.

If you are going to place the tub in a separate shelter, there are several extra factors you will have to consider in addition to the building for an outdoor tub as described in earlier chapters. Wood, double-glazed glass, and rigid plastic are recommended as the most suitable materials for tub enclosures. A general construction book should be consulted for specific building details. The main consideration in cold weather areas is to make sure that the system is really insulated. All pipes and plumbing should be wrapped with black insulating tape; shut-off valves should be installed at the inlet and outlet so that you can drain the plumbing system without emptying the tub.

As to the tub itself, wood is an excellent insulating material, but in severely cold climates some type of insulation around the tub should be added to conserve the heat of the water. The black foam-type blanketing sometimes used in constructing swimming pools would serve well. Ask a pool manufacturer about this. You will want a heavier lid than usually used—the more wood, the better the insulation. Consider either a 2-inch wood lid or a standard lid faced with a layer of foam rubber, also available from pool suppliers.

A close-up view of the indoor wooden tub. Note the expert craftsman-ship of the wooden platform—simple but handsome and convenient as seating and for storing supplies. Photo by Matthew Barr

Hydrojets keep the hot water bubbling and inviting in a sunken wooden tub. Photo by Matthew Barr

9. Maintenance

Keeping your hot tub at peak efficiency requires some periodic maintenance. This does not mean you must be a great mechanic or a whiz with a hammer. It simply means you must keep the water fresh, by cleaning filters and strainers and by adding proper chemicals to the water. Occasionally—about twice a year—you must also drain the tub and refill it with water. None of this is difficult, and once you set up the schedule it becomes a matter of routine.

Water Quality

Preventing the spread of bacteria and controlling algae (which accumulate in water when there is sun) is necessary for any water container, whether it is a swimming pool, a pond, or a hot tub. Chlorine is the chemical that prevents and dissolves these things. Chlorine comes in dry and liquid form; the quantity depends upon how often the tub is used and by how many people. Generally, about 1 cup of chlorine a week is used for a 5-foot diameter tub with water temperature at about 105 degrees. The hotter the water (say, 5 or 10 degrees more) the more chlorine should be used, since heat encourages the growth of bacteria and algae—perhaps one-quarter cup more. Simply pour chlorine from container into water. Allow it to circulate for a few hours before you get into the tub.

Keep the level of acidity or alkalinity in the tub at a neutral level. Use swimming pool test kits (available from suppliers); 7.0 is the neutral zone on the scale. The test kit tests pH, alkalinity, acidity, and chlorine level and comes with a thermometer, chlorine, granular acid, and soda ash. Chlorine has a tendency to make water somewhat acid. If you keep the water at a neutral level and periodically replace any water lost through evaporation and backwashing, you will have to change the water in the tub only twice a year. Test water for balance about once a week.

Chlorine helps keep water clean, but other, new products sold by swimming pool companies also work wonders. Packaged under various trade names, these products are nontoxic biodegradable water cleaners. The solutions gather together small pieces of debris, making them heavy enough to fall to the bottom of the tub, where they are removed by the filter.

Cleaning Equipment

The *filter* for your tub should be cleaned at least twice a month. You can see whether the filter needs cleaning by looking at the clear plastic indicator at the side of the dial valve. To clean the filter, turn off the power switch and move the dial to backwash; next, attach a hose to the drain fitting and turn on power for a few minutes or until the indicator registers clean. Then turn off the power switch and set the dial back to filter.

Clean cartridge filters by turning off the power, removing the filters, and rinsing them with water. Be sure to return them properly so as not to restrict the flow of water.

To *drain the tub* for the semiannual cleaning or whenever you want fresh water in the tub, turn off the power switch and move the dial to drain. Attach a hose to the drain fitting and turn on the power switch. When the tub is drained, fill it with water and add some chlorine (about 1 cup). Then turn the dial valve to recirculate, and turn the power switch on for a minute and then off. While the pump is on recirculate, be sure water is flowing freely into the tub. With the switch off, move the dial valve to filter, and leave it on until the water is heated.

Safety

Always be sure that the immediate area around the hot tub is free of nails, rough wood, and other debris. If the deck or platform is of wood, sand and coat it with plastic coating at the start (Varathane works well).

Keep children's toys away from the tub area. If the tub has a ladder, be sure it is solidly in place. If eating or drinking around the tub, use paper and plastic items to avoid any possible broken glass.

To prevent water from evaporating, as mentioned previously, keep a wooden lid on your tub when it is not in use. The lid also protects children, and grownups, from accidentally falling into the tub, and it keeps the water clean by protecting it from leaves and other debris. Finally, it keeps out cats and other animals, especially on hot summer nights when the creatures get thirsty or nosy.

Unwelcome Guests

You may be thinking this section is about your Uncle Fred or Aunt Fanny. Actually, it is about insects that may be seeking a watering spot as much as you are. Mosquitoes and other pesty insects can be bothersome at evening hours if you are in a hot tub; bees during the day can also add a little annoyance to your life. Some people are tempted to spray the area with noxious chemicals that keep insects away. I would rather put up with the insects because these poisons can enter the water and ultimately affect you.

Whether you use insect preventatives or not is up to you; a better way to avoid the insects is to dunk your head in the tub a second or two until they go away.

10.
How to Use Your Hot Tub

Is there an art to tubbing? Yes, if you want to enjoy the greatest benefits from it. Soaking is good for the mental and physical health, so you should know the correct way to prepare the tub and soak in it. The temperature of the water should be to your liking; the duration of the soaking is up to your personal preference. Towels and a place to dress and undress must also be considered.

Temperature

The water in a hot tub should be good and hot, but an individual's tolerance for heat is a personal thing. For the neophyte a water temperature of 104 degrees is probably fine, but for seasoned hot tub enthusiasts 120 degrees is bliss. For myself, I prefer a range between 105 and 110 degrees; I can sit and soak comfortably in that temperature for about twenty minutes.

The warmer the water, of course, the more it penetrates the body and bones. For example, if you maintain the temperature at 110 degrees, you can probably take only fifteen minutes. If you are socializing, you will want a lower temperature so that you and your guests can stay in the tub longer. However, soaking more than fifteen minutes at high temperatures can be debilitating for some people. It is best to check with your physician to see what soaking time is best for you. (People with heart conditions or other history of poor health should *never* enter a hot tub without the approval of their physicians.)

Like getting into a swimming pool or the ocean, enjoying the hot tub temperature is a matter of acclimating. Do not just plunge in; enter slowly and enjoy the warm relaxation of the tub just as you would sit and enjoy a room of close friends. Soak and absorb, and in a few minutes you will feel your muscles relax and a total easing of tension and strain. Forget your martinis; they will not be necessary and could be harmful. Soaking in water of 105 degrees brings blood to the brain quickly and gives one martini the effect of four. It's better to forget drinking—you won't need it anyway.

Amenities

Have plenty of towels and bathrobes ready for you and your guests when you are finished tubbing—especially in cooler climates. Keep an extra bathing suit or two on hand for modest people who may not wish to soak in the nude.

Oil essences of wintergreen, lemon, and such are available at specialty shops; a few drops of these in the tub create a nice heady effect. Finally, if you drink in the tub (only soft drinks or juices are recommended) get a little floating tray (sold at suppliers), or rig up any type of platform that will allow you to set down plastic glasses.

Soak, inhale the fragrance, look at nature. In sum: Enjoy!

Physical Benefits

Physicians confirm that hot water relaxes tight muscles and dilates blood vessels, thus helping circulation. People with heart trouble and high blood pressure find tubbing a great source of relaxation because the soothing heat of the water relieves tension. (However, people with these conditions should first consult a physician before using a hot tub.) Also, the steam from the hot water greatly enhances skin tone and at the same time rids the pores of poisons and dirt.

Many people find that tubbing helps relieve arthritis, especially in the presence of hydromassage jets; they keep the hot water circulating and thus massage the limbs as well as fingers do. This often helps to reduce pain.

If you have simple back or spine trouble, you will find that after fifteen minutes in a hot tub your back will feel better. Moist heat does the trick; it eases tense and tied-up muscles. And if you suffer from headaches, do not be surprised to find that hot tubbing eases those too.

Many people enjoy a cool shower after a hot soaking, but this is only for the brave. True, the conversion from hot to cold water is invigorating, but it is also a shock to your system and therefore should be done only by seasoned hot tubbers, those who have gradually accustomed themselves to the sudden change in temperatures.

If you are a person who is especially susceptible to colds, use the outdoor hot tub only on mild days. The shock of moving from 105-

degree water into, say, 60-degree air, may render you more susceptible. Have ready suitable towels and a bathrobe to wrap yourself in, and acclimate yourself slowly to the temperature change: start using the tub in warm weather and gradually progress to slightly cooler outdoor temperatures (perhaps by tubbing at night).

There are few things more enjoyable than soaking in a hot tub in the company of good friends. The hot swirling water helps relieve various aches and pains and promotes a general feeling of well-being.
Photo courtesy Pacific Hotbath

Psychological Aspects

Hot tubbing makes you feel good not just physically but emotionally as well. After all, a healthy body promotes a healthy mind, and vice versa. After a good long hot soaking you will find yourself invigorated; any depression you may have felt will have dissolved into the water. The warmth of the water also works wonders on tensions and anxieties and helps to calm worries, leaving you better able to deal with the problems of everyday life.

The social aspect of tubbing with friends is also good for your emotional well-being. There is a closeness in tubs—a sense of community—and we are all social animals. Try to stay angry at a friend in a hot tub; it does not work. Tubbing provides a healthy atmosphere where you can overcome shyness and fear of exposure. There is an openness about the hot tub that is lacking in a conventional small bathroom.

If your tub is outdoors (or even indoors with appropriate surroundings), you will experience a feeling of communing with nature. Sky and plants all meld together with water and you to create a return to the natural and beautiful things. It may sound corny, but it really does produce a sense of peace and harmony that lasts even after you leave the tub.

Sex and the Hot Tub

Many people debunk the hot tub as just a novel setting for engaging in sexual activities. Frankly, you can have sex in your tub, if that is your thing, but the majority of people do not because, put quite simply, after soaking a few minutes in very hot water you are not at your best for physical contact. The heat is far more conducive to relaxation than to activity!

Hot tubs do not lead to orgies or voyeurism. For one thing, people often wear bathing suits while tubbing. As for tubbing in the nude, people may at first feel a certain thrill from looking at unclothed bodies, but after a while we all realize that most of us look better with our clothes on, and the thrill fades. So if you have visions of peeping toms around you, forget it. They will be bored after their first soak.